MEGABRANDS

HOW TO BUILD THEM,
HOW TO BEAT THEM

5/98

Phyllis;

Here's to
our mutual
success in
ruthcare direct
marketing!

John Rayson

MEGABRANDS

HOW TO BUILD THEM
HOW TO BEAT THEM

D. John Loden

IRWIN
Professional Publishing®
Burr Ridge, Illinois
New York, New York

Richard D. Irwin, Inc. recognizes that certain terms in the book are trademarks, and we have made every effort to reprint these throughout the text with the capitalization and punctuation used by the holders of the trademark.

This publication is designed to provide accurate and authoritative information in regard to the subject matter covered. It is sold with the understanding that neither the author nor the publisher is engaged in rendering legal, accounting, or other professional service. If legal advice or other expert assistance is required, the services of a competent professional person should be sought.

From a Declaration of Principles jointly adopted by a Committee of the American Bar Association and a Committee of Publishers.

Sponsoring editor: Cynthia A. Zigmund
Project editor: Rita McMullen
Production manager: Diane Palmer
Jacket Designer: Image House, Inc.
Designer: Larry J. Cope
Compositor: Eastern Graphics
Typeface: 11/13 Palatino
Printer: Arcata Graphics/Kingsport

Library of Congress Cataloging-in-Publication Data

Loden, D. John
    Megabrands : how to build them, how to beat them / by D. John Loden.
       p.   cm.
    ISBN 1-55623-469-4
    1. Product management—United States. 2. Brand name products—United States—Marketing. I. Title.
    HF5415.15.L62 1992
    658.8'27—dc20   91–25048

Printed in the United States of America

1 2 3 4 5 6 7 8 9 0 AGK 8 7 6 5 4 3 2 1

For Marilyn

PREFACE

To borrow a phrase from novelist Joseph Heller, "something happened" to consumer products marketing during the 80s.

At first, these happenings went mostly unnoticed. But as time went on, it became clear that the attitudes and behavior of marketing managers toward major established brands were undergoing a dramatic transformation. Very quickly, these venerable, old products were moving from the background into the limelight. Across corporate America, new product operations were being scaled down, and the focus was shifting to the development of established brands through line extension.

I can't remember the first time I heard one of these dominant brands described as a megabrand, but by 1988, the term seemed to be on everyone's lips. Managers were acutely aware of the increasing importance of these massive products. On an everyday basis, they could see the impact these brands were having on their budgets, on their marketing programs, and even on their organizational structures.

But interestingly, nowhere did there appear to be a formal, well-defined system in place for managing these major product lines. What were the principles of megabrand management? How could the opportunities these products represented be maximized? There seemed to be a growing need to carefully analyze these businesses and better understand how they functioned.

Then one night in March 1990, my wife, Marilyn, and I were having dinner with her editor, Jeffrey Krames from Business One Irwin. Most of the conversation that evening centered on Marilyn's upcoming management book. But at one point, Jeffrey announced that his editorial responsibilities had just been expanded. He told us he would now be responsible for marketing as well as management books. Almost offhandedly, he asked me if I knew anyone who had a good idea in the marketing area.

I mentioned my concept of megabrands, and he seemed interested. Before long, I had written a proposal and it had been accepted. Suddenly, I was confronted with the daunting task of actually writing the manuscript! How was I ever going to fill all those blank pages? But as is often the case, once my attention was directed, I seemed to come across materials on the subject with uncanny frequency. It seemed as though everyday I spotted an article or had a conversation with a colleague that was relevant to the issue. Soon, my conviction that the emergence of megabrands was one of the most significant trends in the marketing world today was confirmed.

But in spite of my strong convictions, writing this book was still a major undertaking that I could never have completed without the support of a number of good friends and associates. I would like to extend my special thanks to Greg Blaine, Bob Ravasio, and Angela Moore-Evans at Foote, Cone & Belding, Lester Barnett, Reg Bowes, and Diane Erickson at Vicom/FCB; and Mike Riley and Craig Sullivan at the Clorox Company for their assistance and thoughtful input.

But most of all, I want to thank my wife, Marilyn, for her unwavering support through all those long evenings and many weekends when I was more than ready to abandon my word processor and go have a beer, and for the many hours she herself spent editing my manuscript and improving my work. Truly, I couldn't have completed this "megatask" without her.

D. John Loden

Contents

INTRODUCTION   xvi

PART 1 A MARKETPLACE IN FLUX   1

CHAPTER 1   THE CHANGING MARKET   3
A Strategy of Acquisition, 4
Merger Mania, 5
Brand Equity, 6
Valuing Brand Equity, 8
    Present Value, 8
    Future Value, 9
    Potential for Line Extension, 9
Market Maturation, 11
Smaller Households, 11
Product Performance, 12
A Game of Inches, 13
Parity Products, 14
Market Segmentation, 15
Segmentation at Work, 16
Market Fragmentation, 17
A Strategy for the 90s, 17
Share Maximization through Line Extension, 18

CHAPTER 2   THE COMING OF THE MEGABRANDS   20
Economy of Scale, 20
The Manufacturing Gap, 21
The Media Gap, 22
Media Inflation, 22
The Advertising Gap, 23
Commercial Clutter, 24
Media Fragmentation, 24
The Sales Promotion Gap, 25
    Rising Promotion Spending, 25

Problems at Retail, 26
The Slotting Allowance, 27
Focus on High-Turn Items, 28
The Technology Gap, 29
Micromarketing, 31
Future Shock, 32
Retreat to Privacy, 34
The Time Crunch, 35

CHAPTER 3   A NEW APPROACH TO MARKETING   38
Dominance, 39
Line of Products, 41
Built around an Established Base Brand, 41
Variations of Core Product Benefit, 42
Marketed in a Consistent and Complementary Manner, 43
Consistent Brand Image, 43
Complementary Marketing Programs, 44
Challenging the Conventional Wisdom, 45
Impact on Brand Image, 46
Line Proliferation, 47
Effect on Customer Base, 48
Impact of Cannibalization, 48
Brand Switching, 48
Potential for Incremental Sales, 48
Implications for Marketing Spending, 49
Ongoing Support, 50
Support Benefit Variation, 50
Opportunities in Related Categories, 51

PART 2
THE PRINCIPLES OF MEGABRAND MANAGEMENT   55

CHAPTER 4   EXPANDING BRAND POSITIONING   57
Importance of Broad Positioning, 57
Reversing the Trend, 58
Systematic Approach, 59
Brand Positioning Defined, 60
Point of Difference as Key Component, 62

Product Benefits, 62
   Understanding the Rational Benefit, 63
   Understanding the Emotional Benefit, 64
   Link to Product Experience, 65
Nonverbal Research Techniques, 66
Emotion in Advertising, 67
Music and Emotion, 68
Expanding Brand Positioning, 70
   Expanding the Rational Benefit, 70
   Enhancing the Emotional Benefit, 72
Brand Character, 74
Brand Symbols, 75

CHAPTER 5   DEVELOPING THE LINE   77
Step 1: Setting the Priorities, 78
   Fill Competitive Gaps, 78
Step 2: Identifying the Opportunities, 80
   Sources of Ideas, 81
   Significance for Megabrands, 86
Step 3: Developing the Products, 86
   Formula Variations, 87
   Aesthetic Variations, 88
   Variations in Product Form, 89
Step 4: Evaluating the Upside, 90
Step 5: Filling the Pipeline, 91
   Life-Style Focus Groups, 92
   Media Analysis, 92

CHAPTER 6   LEVERAGING THE SPENDING   94
Holistic Approach, 95
Common Positioning, 96
Supporting the Existing Line, 97
   Major versus Minor Line Extensions, 98
   Zero-Based Budgeting, 99
   Base-Brand Spending, 100
   Existing Line Extensions, 101
   Computer Modeling, 102
Introducing New Items, 102

The Miracle of Leverage, 103

Advertising, 103

The Halo Effect, 104

Consumer Promotion, 105

Trade Promotion, 106

Timing, 106

A Balancing Act, 108

Avoiding the Pitfalls, 108

CHAPTER 7   EXECUTING THE MARKETING PLAN   110

Micromarketing within the Line, 111

Customized Media, 112

Customized Communications, 113

Coordinating the Plan, 116

The Strategic Business Unit, 117

The Category Manager, 118

Advertising Tactics, 120

Media Tactics, 121

Promotion Tactics, 122

Packaging, 123

Relationship Marketing, 125

CHAPTER 8   MEGABRAND CASE HISTORIES   128

Megahits, 129

Expanding Brand Positioning, 129

Case Study 1: Lysol, 129

Case Study 2: Jell-O, 131

Developing the Line, 132

Case Study 3: Crest, 132

Case Study 4: Coca-Cola, 134

Leveraging the Spending, 135

Case Study 5: Campbell's Soup, 135

Case Study 6: Clorox Bleach, 137

Executing the Plan, 139

Case Study 7: Tide, 139

Case Study 8: Tylenol, 141

Megaflops, 143

Squandering the Spending, 143

Case Study 9: Alka-Seltzer, 143
Confusing Brand Positioning, 144
   Case Study 10: Ban Antiperspirant, 144

PART 3
TAKING ON THE MEGABRANDS BY NICHE MARKETING 149

CHAPTER 9   DEVELOPING NICHE PRODUCTS: A NEW APPROACH 151
Circumventing Megabrand Strengths, 152
Niche Marketing: Conventional Wisdom, 152
Niche Marketing: New Wisdom, 153
Developing Niche Products, 154
   Focused Product Positioning, 155
   Regional Marketing, 157
   Exclusive Channels of Distribution, 159
   Value Pricing, 162
Niche Possibilities, 165

CHAPTER 10   HOW TO MARKET AND MANAGE NICHE PRODUCTS 166
Product Name, 167
Pricing, 167
Media, 169
   Targeted Media, 169
   Regional Media, 170
   Nontraditional Media, 170
Relationship Marketing, 172
Public Relations, 173
Advertising, 173
   Price/Value Advertising, 174
Promotion, 174
   Sampling, 175
   Professional Endorsements, 176
Structural Barriers to Niche Marketing Success, 176
The Acquisition Strategy, 177
Reinventing the Corporation, 178
   Venture Groups, 178
New Skills and New Mind-Sets, 181

CHAPTER 11   NICHE MARKETING CASE HISTORIES   183
                 Niche Marketing Hits, 184
                 Focused Product Positioning, 184
                     Case Study 1: Healthy Choice, 184
                     Case Study 2: Tilex, 185
                 Regional Marketing, 187
                     Case Study 3: Celestial Seasonings, 187
                     Case Study 4: Murphy's Oil Soap, 188
                 Exclusive Channels of Distribution, 190
                     Case Study 5: Interplak, 190
                     Case Study 6: Metamucil, 190
                 Value Pricing, 193
                     Case Study 7: Barbasol, 193
                     Case Study 8: ScotTowels, 195
                 NICHE MARKETING FLOPS, 196
                 No Product Difference, 197
                 No Consumer Demand, 197
                 Poor Product Performance, 199
                 Range of Activity, 199

PART 4 MEGABRANDS AND THE FUTURE   201

CHAPTER 12   MEGABRANDS AND THE FUTURE   203
                 Multinational Competitors, 204
                 New-Product Source, 205
                 Europe 1992, 206
                     Common Advertising, 207
                     Shared Media, 208
                 Asia, 208
                     Japan, 209
                     China, 210
                 Global Megabrands, 210
                 Global Product Standardization, 211
                 Megabrands on the Home Front, 212
                     Emphasis on Line Extension, 213
                     Shorter New-Product Life Cycles, 213
                 Marketing in the Next Millennium, 214

Hypertargeting, 214
Selective Media, 215
Selective Promotion, 215
Product Technology, 216
From Global to Personal, 217
The New Reality, 218

INDEX   220

Introduction

Always a difficult task, successful new-product development became even more challenging during the 1980s.

Through the decade U.S. corporations lost billions of dollars in unsuccessful attempts to introduce new brand names into the consumer marketplace.

According to industry lore, only 1 new product in 100 made it successfully through test markets into national distribution. Of these, only 1 in 10 achieved annual sales of $15 million or more.

The actual statistics may be even more severe. In a speech to the American Marketing Association, Herb Baum, president of the Campbell Soup Company, stated, "Only 4 percent of all new products reach the $20 million sales level and only 0.5 percent make the $100 million mark."[1]

Discouraging figures were also reported by *New Product News*, a trade publication that studies new product activity in food stores. According to these estimates, "Some 10,182 new products (defined as new brands or line extensions) were introduced in 1987, and the 1988 crop is estimated at close to 11,000. . . . The failure rate [is] estimated at 80 percent. That's far too high when you consider it might take $35 to $45 million to launch a new product on a wide scale."[2]

The reasons behind these brand failures are linked to a variety of demographic, economic, and marketplace factors. But regardless of the causes, there is no doubt the high-risk game of new-brand development became even riskier in the decade just past. In fact, for many manufacturers the risks appeared so high that the game didn't seem worth playing at all. Fortunately an alternative was at hand.

At the same time corporations were struggling so desperately in the new-product arena, many were experiencing unprecedented success with their established products.

In many of the largest consumer products categories, the number 1 brand from 1980 was still in the top spot 10 years later. In fact, many had actually strengthened their leadership positions.

Unhappily, this good fortune wasn't shared by all established brand-name products. Throughout the 80s the polarization phenomenon evident in society at large was also apparent in the world of product marketing. Like the ranks of the middle class, the ranks of the mid-size brands shrank during this period. As this shrinkage occurred, the middle began to disappear and brand franchises began to gravitate to the extremes of large and small.

For the "haves" in product marketing, as in society at large, the 80s proved to be a very good decade indeed. It was a time of consolidation and gain. The rich got richer and the big got bigger. So big, in fact, that a new prefix entered the popular lexicon to describe the titanic dimensions of their success. Their descriptor was *mega* and soon it was being used everywhere to connote super-large scale.

Heralded by the publication of John Naisbitt's *Megatrends* in 1982, the 80s became the decade of the megaphenomenon. During this period America was introduced to a succession of new words to describe these vast realities. Terms like megahits, megamergers, and *megabucks* quickly became part of the popular vernacular. And somewhere in the corridors of corporate America, a now forgotten marketer coined the expression *megabrand*.

A *megabrand*, as the term is generally used by marketers today, is one of an elite group of consumer franchises with a loyal, massive, and growing customer base.

With the competitive environment projected to intensify during the 1990s, there is little doubt that the dominance of megabrands will continue to grow. Therefore, understanding how to develop, manage, and compete against megabrands will be absolutely critical to marketing success.

For those responsible for major product lines, this knowledge will be essential in any efforts aimed at building large brands into megabrands. For those in charge of smaller products, a knowledge of megabrand marketing will be required to understand the vulnerabilities of these products and to prosper in the face of massive competition. In short, a working knowledge of megabrand marketing will be a prerequisite for virtually all marketing professionals.

Like any aspect of marketing, the insights and skills necessary to succeed in this new competitive era can be analyzed, mastered, and applied. This book has been designed to provide the perspectives and skills necessary to compete successfully in the decade ahead.

Part 1 of this book examines the changing market conditions that set the stage for the emergence of the megabrand. In this section megabrands are defined and the megabrand approach to marketing is contrasted with more traditional practices.

In Part 2 the principles of successful megabrand management are discussed. Specific topics include:

1. Expanding brand positioning.
2. Developing the product line.
3. Leveraging the spending.
4. Executing the marketing plan.

Part 3 contains an in-depth consideration of niche marketing, a potent counterstrategy to the megabrand onslaught. The review covers the most popular niche marketing approaches and provides a number of concrete tips for niche marketing success.

To graphically illustrate the principles of both megabrand marketing and niche marketing, Parts 2 & 3 also feature a series of consumer product case histories. In addition to success stories, several notable failures are showcased to highlight common mistakes and pitfalls.

Finally, in Part 4, the focus shifts to the future with a discussion of where tomorrow's megabrands will be likely to appear and a consideration of the role that megabrands are destined to play in our developing global economy.

As we race toward the next millennium, the parameters of tomorrow's consumer marketplace are already taking shape. Trends that began in the 1980s will gain greater momentum as we move into the 1990s. In the fast-changing, competitive world of marketing, there can be no going back to the comfortable approaches of the past. Future shock is a fact of contemporary life.

For marketers unable to deal with the stresses of this new environment, the time has come to consider a career change or early retirement. But for those marketers who understand the new realities and are willing to act on this knowledge, the opportunities will be enormous. The era of the megabrand will offer vast, new rewards.

NOTES

1. Judann Dagnoli, "Cooling Down," *Advertising Age*, March 2, 1987, p. 69.
2. "New Products: The Fatal Attraction," *New Product News*, December 9, 1988, p. 8.

PART 1

A MARKETPLACE IN FLUX

Chapter One

The Changing Market

Let's begin by going back.

It's the summer of 1982. Julie and Bill Miller, a young, working couple, are about to begin their weekly food shopping. Bill pulls a cart from the stack in front of the neighborhood Safeway and they enter the store. As they move down aisle 1, Julie removes a shopping list from her purse. Slowly their basket begins to fill up with familiar items.

For breakfast there's Post Raisin Bran, a can of Maxwell House coffee, and a fresh Dole pineapple. For lunch, they choose some Oscar Mayer cold cuts, a package of Velveeta cheese, and a jar of Kraft mayonnaise. And for dinner, an assortment of Lean Cuisine frozen entrees, Birds Eye Gourmet Vegetables, and Pillsbury Ready-to-Serve Rolls. For the weekend cookout, they pick up a six-pack of Miller beer and two cans of Planters nuts. Then a quick turn down the health and beauty aids aisle produces a box of Bayer aspirin, some Flex shampoo, and a bottle of Pepto-Bismol.

Julie pauses for a moment and checks her watch. She's pleased to see their shopping is progressing nicely. At this rate, she and Bill should have no trouble making their 10 o'clock tennis date. Looking over the list one last time, the Millers proceed toward the checkout counter.

Now let's move the clock forward by 10 years. The decade of the 80s is over and the world has changed dramatically. Ronald Reagan has come and gone. The Iran hostage crisis has been replaced by a new Middle East crisis. Drug use is rising, and for many Americans, quality of life is falling. In addition the cost of living continues to increase. Economic recovery has cycled back into recession, and day-to-day existence has become more stressful and complex.

Now it's a Saturday morning in July 1992, and Julie and Bill Miller are once again engaged in their weekly shopping ritual. In their mid-30s the Millers are still an attractive couple, although both look tired from their hectic office schedules. Sitting happily in the shopping cart is Catherine, their three-year-old daughter. Catherine goes everywhere with them on the weekends since they have so little "quality time" with her during the week.

As Julie begins her shopping routine, it's remarkable how little her purchase habits have been affected by all the changes that have taken place over the past 10 years. Aisle by aisle, she still reaches for many of the same, familiar brand names. But while Julie may think she's buying the same products, these brands are different in one very important respect.

What Julie doesn't realize is that each of the brands she's selected has been acquired by new owners over the past 10 years. In some cases products have changed hands more than once. Even her supermarket, the neighborhood Safeway, was bought by management in a leveraged buyout then resold to the public in a major stock offering.

As remarkable as it seems, the average consumer was largely oblivious to these massive transfers of brand ownership. Yet it was the purchase habits of average people like Julie that provided the impetus for these major transactions. For it was in the consistent buying behavior of these consumers that financial experts began to recognize a tangible, highly desirable financial asset.

A STRATEGY OF ACQUISITION

The concept of branding is nothing new. Brands, as we know them today, have been around since the 19th century when they were created by manufacturers to differentiate one product from another and to ensure the purchaser of a product's quality. As a result there has always been a substantial dollar value inherent in a brand name. However, in recent years, that value has increased dramatically.

During the 1980s Wall Street speculators reached a collective realization. After decades of inflation, analysts correctly perceived that it would be far less costly long-term to acquire an established franchise (even at a super-premium price) than build a business from the ground up. Beyond cost considerations, there was the uncertainty of launching a new business in an increasingly uncertain economic climate. In an era when the rate of new-product failure was appalling, the risks of new-brand development seemed unacceptably high.

As a result Wall Street came to appreciate the tremendous financial value of the existing relationships that established brands enjoyed with consumers. They recognized that the strong loyalty consumers felt toward familiar products could be translated into concrete assets with cash values as real as warehouse inventories and plant equipment. A new term, *brand equity*, appeared in marketing parlance to describe a brand's intangible assets in the marketplace. Backed by easy junk-bond financing, speculators set out to acquire the prized equities of major consumer brands.

MERGER MANIA

As one acquisition led to another, a veritable feeding frenzy began to develop. Fearing they'd lose out, corporate raiders, investment bankers, and inside deal makers engaged in cutthroat bidding wars that drove the prices of consumer products companies into the stratosphere. Each day it seemed a new takeover was announced, each time at a record price. Driven on by the prospect of windfall profits, Wall Street fell into a state of mass buying psychosis that the press dubbed *merger mania*.

Throughout the 1980s, businesses changed hands on a previously unheard of scale. According to *Mergers & Acquisitions* magazine, over 31,000 transactions took place during the decade. This translated to roughly 250 deals per month or a mind-boggling eight deals per day! The aggregate value of these transactions was $1.34 trillion.[1] Of this total amount, a high percentage was spent to acquire consumer products companies.

In fact consumer products companies were the focus of five of the biggest deals of the 80s, culminating in the largest acquisition in Wall Street history—the $25 billion leveraged buyout of

RJR/Nabisco. It began with the management buyout of Beatrice Foods for $6.2 billion. This was followed in 1985 by the $5.75 billion acquisition of General Foods by Philip Morris. In 1988 Philip Morris added Kraft Foods to its list of subsidiaries for the price of $11 billion. Also in 1988 the British conglomerate Grand Metropolitan acquired Pillsbury in a hostile takeover. Then finally in 1989, there was the massive $25 billion RJR/Nabisco buyout.

In these five deals alone, the ownership of hundreds of major brands changed hands, including some of the best-known trademarks in American business. On the list were names like Maxwell House coffee, Jell-O gelatin, Philadelphia Cream Cheese, Breyers ice cream, Planters peanuts, Ritz crackers, Kool-Aid, and Hawaiian Punch—just to mention a few. The prices these consumer products companies commanded defied all the traditional valuation formulas based on calculating the worth of tangible assets. Clearly the intangible asset of brand equity was having a major influence on purchase price.

BRAND EQUITY

In discussing a recent acquisition, the vice president of marketing of Cadbury Schweppes referred directly to the high value of these intangible assets. Commenting on the $220 million price that his company paid to Procter & Gamble for the Hires and Crush soft-drink lines, he remarked, "Some $20 million [of the price] was for physical assets: the rest was for brand value."[2]

A similar appreciation of the value of the intangible aspects of brand equity was reflected in a recent speech by another top marketing executive. Addressing a group of industry professionals, the executive vice president of a top, international food company, put it simply, "You don't buy assets, you buy brands."[3]

But what exactly is this asset called *brand equity* that seems to be on every marketer's lips and for which investors are willing to pay such high prices? How is it different from the product itself? During the past several years both academics and business professionals have attempted to develop a precise definition. Peter H. Farquhar, director of the Center for Product Research at Carnegie-Mellon University's Graduate School of Industrial Administration, has made a careful study of this subject.

According to Farquhar, "Brand equity is the added value that a brand endows on a product. That something extra. We need to distinguish between the product and the brand. The product is something that has a functional purpose. . . . The brand is the name, symbol, design, or mark that enhances the value of that product beyond its functional purpose."[4]

A slightly different but consistent perspective is provided by marketing consultant Allen McCusker. According to McCusker, brand equity is

> the dollar value marketing and time have built in the years the brand has been used and experienced by consumers. . . . A brand's equity emanates from the personal interaction a consumer has with the brand. This includes stimuli from advertising messages, childhood memories, experiences, family usage, etc. These relationships are both intellectual and emotional. . . .
>
> When we define a brand's equity we give it life in nonproduct terms. We unearth what the brand stands for, not what the product is. The specific attributes we use to describe a product—size, shape, color, texture—are not the brand. The brand is the imagery built around the product as a base.[5]

To illustrate this point, let's return one last time to Julie Miller and her shopping cart. If someone were to question Julie about her motives for brand purchase, she would no doubt mention such logical reasons as product quality and reliability. She might cite the fact that she can rely on these products to deliver their promised benefits consistently over time.

But if one were to probe more deeply, Julie would probably reveal some less rational motives. She might describe these brands as trusted and reliable friends. She might tell you these products were family traditions—"products that my mother used." In a very real sense, Julie would be describing a personal, emotional relationship between herself and these products. Clearly, feelings like these contribute greatly to the value of well-known brands. But how does one begin to place dollar value on such ethereal characteristics?

VALUING BRAND EQUITY

Calculating the dollar value of brand equity has been the subject of intense discussion in the marketing and financial communities. At this stage, no definitive, universally accepted formula has been developed. However, it is clear that a true valuation must take into account both the present and future worth of these intangible assets.

An accurate formula must analyze these values from at least three critical perspectives:

1. The present value of the price premium the brand name commands in the marketplace.
2. The future value of a large, stable franchise.
3. The opportunities such a franchise will provide for line extension in the future.

Present Value

Key to estimating the present value of brand equity is the ability to distinguish between the tangible value of the product itself and the intangible value that is added through brand name association. Carnegie-Mellon's Peter Farquhar describes one approach for attacking this problem:

> From the firm's perspective, brand equity can be measured by the incremental cash flow from associating the brand with the product. . . . In matched product tests with corn flakes cereal, choice increased from 47 percent when the brand name was not known to 59 percent when the Kellogg's brand name was identified. . . . The increased market share from the brand can be readily translated into a dollar measure of equity.

But as Farquhar points out, factors beyond differences in absolute market share must also be considered when calculating the present value of brand equity. He continues,

> Incremental cash flow also results from premium pricing and reduced promotional expenses. Coopers & Lybrand evaluates brand equity by comparing the premium price commanded by a branded product with the price of unbranded products. Arthur Young assesses the profitability of a branded versus an unbranded product

by accounting for advertising, trademark registration, and other expenses of branding. These refinements offer a more accurate measure of a brand's equity.[6]

At this point, it seems unlikely that a standard formula for calculating the present value of brand equity will be agreed upon any time soon. But one thing is certain—getting a better grip on the key components of brand equity has been given a high priority in financial marketing circles today and will continue to be a subject of great debate for years to come.

Future Value

Apart from present worth, a valuation of a brand's equity must consider the product's future volume potential. History has shown that major, established franchises have incredible psychological staying power with consumers that translates into vast, untapped earnings potential. Like a piece of prime real estate, a prime brand is virtually guaranteed to increase in worth over the years.

The American Association of Advertising Agencies recently published the results of a study that attests to the lasting value of consumer-brand relationships. The analysis revealed that "in 19 of 22 consumer categories, the leading brand of the year 1925 was still the leader 60 years later"![7] The brands by category are listed in Table 1–1.

In light of current marketplace conditions, there is good reason to believe that the position of major, established brands such as these will grow even stronger. By applying even a conservative scenario that assumes only stable sales, the future values of these leading brands, based on inflation alone, will be prodigious.

Potential for Line Extension

Finally, valuing brand equity must take into account another dimension of future worth. This additional dimension is the platform the brand provides for growth through line extension. Today's marketplace is openly hostile to most new products; but it is extremely receptive to major brand-line extension. This market prejudice in favor of line extensions is underscored by the results of a recent survey which found that "89 percent of new consumer

TABLE 1–1
The Leading Brands: 1925 and 1985

	Leading Brand 1925	Current Position 1985
Bacon	Swift	Leader
Batteries	Eveready	Leader
Biscuits	Nabisco	Leader
Breakfast cereal	Kellogg	Leader
Cameras	Kodak	Leader
Canned fruit	Del Monte	Leader
Chewing gum	Wrigley	Leader
Chocolates	Hershey	No. 2
Flour	Gold Medal	Leader
Mint candies	Life Savers	Leader
Paint	Sherwin-Williams	Leader
Pipe tobacco	Prince Albert	Leader
Razors	Gillette	Leader
Sewing machines	Singer	Leader
Shirts	Manhattan	No. 5
Shortening	Crisco	Leader
Soap	Ivory	Leader
Soft drinks	Coca-Cola	Leader
Soup	Campbell's	Leader
Tea	Lipton	Leader
Tires	Goodyear	Leader
Toothpaste	Colgate	No. 2

product introductions were line extensions, 6 percent were category extensions, and only 5 percent were new brands."[8] In this context a brand's ability to serve as a launching pad for future line extensions is another financial asset that must be considered when valuing brand equity.

Certainly, the potential for future line extensions has always been an important factor when calculating the value of brand equity. But in recent years, the estimated value of such line extensions has risen exponentially as changing market conditions have made the successful development of new brands progressively more difficult. These changes have involved three distinct but interrelated developments:

1. Market maturation.
2. Market segmentation.
3. Market fragmentation.

Each has played a major role in creating the market situation that exists today. Each, in its own way, has changed the rules of the marketing game. Each has tilted the balance away from new products in favor of existing brands.

MARKET MATURATION

The years of economic expansion following World War II were marked by an explosion in population growth and a related explosion in the growth of consumer product markets. At the conclusion of the war, new households were formed at an unprecedented rate. These households quickly began producing offspring, and before long the baby boom had shifted into high gear. These millions of growing, child-oriented households became the heaviest users of a host of new and traditional packaged goods products. They also became the prime target group for thousands of American companies.

With so many high-consumption households to sell to, business boomed. Each year, categories and the brands within them simply got bigger. These "wonder years" continued through the 1960s as the baby boom generation grew and matured. But by the mid-70s, business began to slow appreciably. The baby boomers had abandoned the nest and were waiting longer to start their own households. In time most "boomers" did marry and begin their own families. But their families tended to include fewer children than those of the previous generation. This was bad news for marketers.

SMALLER HOUSEHOLDS

According to Census Bureau statistics, the average size of the U.S. household shrank appreciably in the 20 years between 1960 and 1980.[9] This trend is illustrated in the following table.

Average Household Size

	Number of Persons
1960	3.33
1970	3.14
1980	2.76
1989	2.62

In addition more recent Census Bureau studies point to an increase in a related demographic category—the number of households with no children at all. According to the latest census data, only 26 percent of married couple households had children under 18 in 1990 compared to 31 percent in 1980.[10] From a demographic standpoint, the U.S. population has moved out of a period of hypergrowth into a more stable, mature phase.

PRODUCT PERFORMANCE

The same maturity that began to characterize American consumers also began to characterize American consumer products. As time marched on, the performance advantages that once distinguished one brand from another began to disappear. As products themselves moved into middle age, many seemed to lose their uniqueness and converge into a homogeneous mass. In a competitive marketplace, this had to spell trouble.

From the beginning of the mass marketing era, smart marketers have realized that the best way to ensure product success is to provide superior performance over competitive brands. Whether the category is mousetraps or mustards, they know consumers will beat a path to their door if they can provide a better product. In the mid-70s, what marketers had always known intuitively about the importance of product superiority was substantiated through quantitative research.

In a landmark study published in the *Harvard Business Review*, marketing executive J. Hugh Davidson documented the advantages and disadvantages of launching a new brand without a significant performance advantage. In an article entitled, "Why Most

New Consumer Brands Fail," Davidson stated, "Fully 74 percent of the successes I studied offered the consumer better performance at the same or a higher price, while only 20 percent of the failures fitted this category. At the same or a higher price, the vast majority of failures (80%) had the same performance as the other brands already on the market."[11]

A summary of Davidson's research findings is shown in Table 1–2.

Davidson's findings, along with the results of similar studies, have confirmed that product superiority isn't something that is simply nice to have. It's an absolutely essential ingredient in new product success. Its presence or absence can literally make or break any new brand.

A GAME OF INCHES

Within consumer product categories, developing new products that provide superior performance has always been a game of inches. Today the challenge has become even more difficult. Patent protection for most product technologies expired years ago and new technological breakthroughs are few and far between. In recent years the situation has been further complicated by the fact that basic consumer needs in most product categories have already been met.

With consumers largely satisfied with the performance of

TABLE 1–2
Successes and Failures of 50 New Brands

Difference from Competitors	Of 50 Successes	Of 50 Failures
Significantly Better Performance/Higher Price	44	8
Marginally Better Performance/Higher Price	6	12
Better Performance/Same Price	24	0
Same Performance/Lower Price	8	0
Same Performance/Same Price	16	30
Same Performance/Higher Price	2	30
Worse Performance/Same or Higher Price	0	20
Total	100	100

their brands and essentially the same technologies available to everyone, marketers have had to concentrate on developing products with only minor performance improvements. Still, by being first to the market with these products, they have been able to gain significant advantage. In the months or years it takes the competition to respond, the innovating company is often able to build a significant franchise.

But by the end of the 1980s, the world of marketing, like the world at large, was reeling from a heavy dose of future shock. Computers and robotized manufacturing facilities had made it possible to rapidly duplicate product innovations without extended lead times. As a result, innovators could no longer count on long periods of market exclusivity for their new products. On the contrary it became extremely difficult to maintain product differences for more than a few months.

Today, if a new product demonstrates any consumer vitality, it's certain that copy-cat products will quickly follow. In fact, there are even instances where the innovating company has been preempted by a quick-footed competitor. The scenario goes as follows. The competitor picks up the innovation while the original product is still in test market. Then, by introducing its own version nationally, the competition preempts the innovator and claims the product as its own.

PARITY PRODUCTS

Today marketers operate in an environment of parity products where comparable brands deliver comparable benefits and competitive advantages are fleeting at best. What's more, product similarities are not lost on consumers. In a recent Roper survey, a national sample of consumers agreed that "there were little differences between premium brands and other brands."[12]

If this situation weren't difficult enough, the new-product marketer's job today has been made even more challenging by the growing ineffectiveness of market segmentation—the technique that has served as the marketer's primary tool for overcoming the problem of product similarities for over 30 years. Throughout the professional lifetimes of most modern-day managers, market segmentation has been at the center of all new-product development activities. It has been the most effective antidote for curing the malaise of product sameness. But today that antidote appears to be losing much of its potency.

MARKET SEGMENTATION

According to the principle of market segmentation, consumer categories should not be thought of as monolithic. Instead, they should be conceived as interrelated segments. Each of these segments is discrete and is defined by specific consumer needs. By precisely identifying these needs, marketers can develop specialized products that satisfy these wants more satisfactorily than preexisting products with more general positionings and a broader range of applications.

The revolutionary insight provided by the market segmentation theory is that minor brand differences can have a major impact on brand sales. Even though segmented products might vary only slightly from competitive brands, they can still be very appealing to the distinct groups for which they were created. To the manager utilizing market segmentation, a consumer category is like a pie that can be cut into many slices. The trick, of course, lies in knowing where to cut!

To assist managers with the task of market segmentation, researchers invented a technique known as *need gap analysis*. Need gap analysis is essentially a two-step process. The first step breaks down a particular market into a hierarchy of consumer needs and wants; the second step measures how satisfactorily these needs are being met by currently available products. Where a gap exists between a stated need and the level of consumer satisfaction with current products, there may well lie a new-product opportunity.

With the addition of some old-fashioned intuition and basic imagination, the technique of market segmentation through need gap analysis spawned decades of product innovations and drove growth in the U.S. marketplace. By precisely identifying consumer wants, marketers were able to introduce successions of new-product modifications that provided improved performance against finely defined wants. Market segmentation was so successful, it was quickly and universally adopted and applied across all product categories.

SEGMENTATION AT WORK

The over-the-counter pain reliever category serves as a classic example of the role that market segmentation played in developing new products that address specific consumer needs. Until the 1960s, the pain reliever market was thought of as monolithic, with all products delivering the same benefit—effective pain relief. Moreover, one ingredient—aspirin—in a single, standard dosage was perceived to effectively satisfy all consumer needs.

Then, influenced by market segmentation, companies realized that the general benefit of effective pain relief could be broken down into a number of more specific benefits based upon more precise consumer wants. As new products were created to satisfy these wants, distinct market segments began to emerge. The first segment to appear was "extra strength," with Anacin offering greater potency than regular aspirin. Then a "safety" segment emerged with Bufferin promising fast relief without stomach upset.

It wasn't long before these new segments were themselves split apart. In the extra-strength segment, Anacin was joined by Excedrin, which offered extra-strength relief for a specific symptom—headache. In the safety segment, Bufferin was joined by Tylenol, which offered safety with no aspirin side effects.

Over the next two decades, the process continued. More segments were created by defining more specialized needs (e.g., extra-strength products for arthritis). Eventually the market was so completely and carefully dissected that trying to find a significant, unfulfilled need was like trying to find a needle in a haystack.

The pattern of segmentation in the analgesic market is representative of what has occurred in every consumer product category during the 60s and 70s. Today each of these markets has been cut into pieces so thin that little substance is left to carve up. What's more, the small segments that still remain do not represent enough volume potential to justify the massive expenditures necessary to introduce a new brand.

By the 1980s the strategy of new-brand development based upon market segmentation had simply run out of steam. Market segments had turned into market fragments that weren't large enough to sustain major new brands. Manufacturers that chose to ignore this reality and assume a business-as-usual approach paid dearly for their arrogance with major new-product failures.

MARKET FRAGMENTATION

But in every crisis, there is also opportunity. While market fragmentation was devastating for new-brand development, it presented exciting growth opportunities for line extensions of existing brands. While large numbers of consumers weren't anxiously awaiting the next major brand of pain reliever or laundry detergent, there were smaller groups still very interested in minor innovations that provided secondary benefits, like easy-to-swallow coated tablets or environmentally safe packages. What's more, these groups were willing to pay a premium price for the extra advantages.

Although the absolute numbers of consumers interested in these secondary innovations weren't large enough to sustain new, independent franchises, they were more than adequate to support line extensions of existing franchises. Consequently, line extensions began to appear at an accelerating rate throughout the 1980s. As they did, it became apparent that the classic marketing formulas that had worked so well in the past were no longer effective in this highly fragmented marketplace.

A STRATEGY FOR THE 90s

As the dust settled from the 1980s, it was clear that many things had permanently changed. Merger mania had run its course. As the debt crisis worsened, the bloom was off the junk-bond rose. Like Michael Milken, takeovers, hostile or otherwise, were quickly becoming an artifact of the past. In the new decade of the 90s, corporate growth through acquisition was no longer a viable approach.

Likewise, a strategy of corporate growth through new-brand

introduction was no longer workable. Market segmentation—the strategy that had stimulated new-brand growth throughout the 60s and 70s—had lost its effectiveness and couldn't be revived. For consumer product businesses to grow in the 90s, a new strategy was desperately needed. Fortunately for some, that strategy was at hand.

Just as market segmentation had been the predominant strategy of the 60s and 70s and brand acquisition the preferred approach during the 80s, growth through the line extension would prove to be the strategy for the 1990s. Those marketers in the best position to take advantage of this new reality were the owners of large, established brands.

SHARE MAXIMIZATION THROUGH LINE EXTENSION

Because of the dominant positions these products held in the marketplace, major brands were best situated to turn the tide of market fragmentation to their advantage. For a variety of reasons that will be examined throughout this book, these already dominant brands were best equipped to increase their shares even more through aggressive line extension. As overall market growth continued to slow, share maximization became the watchword.

Suddenly, marketers began to see their established businesses in a new light. They were no longer cash cows to be milked in support of new-brand introductions. Nor were they simply financial instruments approaching maturity and ready to be sold. They were, in fact, the very heart of consumer product companies, the engines capable of pumping a continuous flow of lifegiving energy and revenue into mature corporations. As such, they represented the primary source of renewal and growth.

After years in the background, established brands once again moved to center stage. A light bulb went on in the minds of marketers. The growth strategy of the 1990s wasn't market expansion via new brands nor was it the acquisition of existing franchises. It was share maximization through the line extension of existing brands! In an era of global consolidation, the most viable marketing strategy would be one that reflected the trends taking place in the world at large. The biggest brands were destined to get bigger.

With this realization the course was set. The sizable resources of consumer products companies—time, money, brainpower—would be set toward the accomplishment of this objective. It was now only a matter of time. The superbrands of today were destined to become the megabrands of tomorrow.

NOTES

1. Edward T. O'Toole, "Mergers and Acquisitions: 1990 Annual Report," *Barron's*, July 23, 1990, p. 28.
2. Howard Schlossberg, "Brand Value Can Be Worth More than Physical Assets," *Marketing News*, March 5, 1990, p. 6.
3. Camillo Pagano, Foote, Cone & Belding Worldwide Management Conference, Laguna Niguel, California, June 1990.
4. Peter H. Farquhar, "Brand Equity—The Attitude That Ties It All Together," AMA Attutide Research Conference, Orlando, Florida, January 29– February 1, 1989.
5. Allen McCusker, "Brand Equity: What It Is and What to Do with It," *Food & Beverage Marketing*, May 1990, p. 59.
6. Peter H. Farquhar, "Managing Brand Equity," *Marketing Research*, September 1989, p. 24.
7. Committee on the Value of Advertising, American Association of Advertising Agencies, "The Value Side of Productivity: A Key to Competitive Survival in the 1990s," 1989, p. 18.
8. Edward F. Ogiba, "The Dangers of Leveraging," *Adweek*, January 4, 1988, p. 42.
9. U.S. Bureau of the Census, *Current Population Reports*, series P-25, no. 986, p. 45.
10. Judith Waldrop and Thomas Exter, "The Legacy of the 1980s," *American Demographics*, March 1991, p. 33.
11. J. Hugh Davidson, "Why Most New Consumer Brands Fail," *Harvard Business Review*, March–April 1976, p. 119.
12. "Consumers in Recession," *The Public Pulse*, November 1, 1990, Section 1, p. 1.

Chapter Two

The Coming of the Megabrands

Looking back at the media coverage of the 1980s, one could easily assume this was the decade of the entrepreneur. Month after month, year after year, the faces of successful, young company founders graced the covers of America's leading business and news publications. In reading their success stories, it often seemed that the era of big business was coming to an end. The country appeared on the verge of abandoning large corporations and returning to its individualistic roots.

No doubt the 80s did witness a resurgence of entrepreneurial activity in some industries. But a stronger and far more significant trend was also occurring, and it was moving in exactly the opposite direction. Beyond anything else, the 80s were a time of consolidation of economic and marketing power within major corporations and major product lines. Propelling this trend was a renewed demand for greater efficiency and productivity and, beneath it all, the need to achieve the critical mass that would generate economies of scale.

ECONOMY OF SCALE

During the 1980s, economy of scale became the operative principle in every area of marketing. In America's mature consumer markets, managers again saw that absolute size bestowed a wide range of competitive advantages. But in one important respect, the contemporary definition of *mass* was different from earlier conceptions. This time the definition was holistic. It recognized mass as not simply a monolithic whole, but as the sum of distinct, interdependent parts.

During periods of rapid market growth, successful companies are primarily distinguished by their ability to innovate—to create new products and new approaches. But in slow-growth markets, where share maximization is the name of the game, the benefits of absolute size take on greater significance. Throughout the 1980s, marketers began to recognize and exploit economies of scale across the entire gamut of manufacturing, marketing, and sales. In the process, consumer markets began to polarize and gaps appeared to widen between large and small brands.

THE MANUFACTURING GAP

Historically the advantages of scale have been most apparent in the production realm. In bargaining for raw materials, manufacturers purchasing the greatest quantities have often been able to negotiate the lowest prices. Likewise, manufacturers of products with large consumer franchises were usually able to keep high-speed manufacturing lines operating at maximum efficiency, while smaller competitors suffered frequent and costly periods of downtime.

In addition major manufacturers could spread the substantial fixed costs of plant and equipment over a larger volume base. Since absolute costs were often comparable for big and small competitors, smaller companies were placed at a severe cost disadvantage. This disadvantage often translated to higher, less competitive prices at retail.

Finally, the economic efficiencies of high volume gave savvy competitors the financial ballast required to continuously modernize their manufacturing facilities and invest heavily in research and development. The cumulative effect of this modernization and R&D investment, particularly in today's high-tech age, has at times created such huge discrepancies in production capabilities and product performance that many smaller companies have been literally forced to withdraw from the market.

THE MEDIA GAP

Economies of scale have not been limited exclusively to the manufacturing sector. In the 1980s the advantages of size became more
apparent in advertising, promotion, and sales as well. The benefits of size were a direct function of the high levels of absolute
spending required to compete in major consumer categories. In
the realm of consumer advertising, size was a powerful determinant in separating the nonplayers from those who could afford to
harness the most powerful and pervasive communications force
in society—television.

Throughout the postwar era, network television has been the
media engine driving the consumer products marketing machine.
This quintessential mass medium has provided the perfect showcase for products targeted at large, national audiences. In the
beginning, because of the networks' low cost per thousand
(viewers), national brand marketers could afford to advertise their
products throughout the year. As such, they were able to maintain constant visibility for their brands in categories where purchases were frequent and top-of-mind awareness was critical to
success.

To some degree major brands with more money to spend
always enjoyed purchasing advantages over smaller competitors.
However, through the 1970s, the cost of network TV was within
reach of most national brands. The majority could afford to purchase network schedules large enough to generate adequate
reach and frequency in their target audiences on a year-round
basis. Armed with effective advertising copy, they could still compete effectively against the big boys.

MEDIA INFLATION

But in the 1980s severe media inflation began to seriously restrict
the ability of smaller products to communicate their stories to
their mass targets. As network prices soared, many marketers
found themselves unable to afford a "basic" year-round network
schedule. Instead, some were forced to reduce their schedules to
dangerously low levels or even abandon year-round advertising
and concentrate their spending during specific periods.

Throughout the 1980s the price of commercial airtime on the country's three major networks rose at a rate significantly higher than overall inflation. According to an article in *Forbes* magazine, "In 1980 the average price for 30 seconds of prime time on the networks was $63,800. Thirty seconds of network prime time today goes for an average of $112,600. That's a 76 percent jump in prices."[1]

Concealed within the "average costs" were the astronomical costs of time on the most popular, highly rated network programs. For example, during the 1990–91 season, the price of a 30-second spot on hit shows like "The Simpsons," "Roseanne," or "The Bill Cosby Show" ranged from $300,000 to $400,000.[2] But even these prices pale when compared to the most expensive program of them all—the Super Bowl. In 1989 the average cost of a 30-second spot on the NFL championship game was an astounding $800,000.[3]

While the rising cost of network television time eroded the buying power of advertisers across the board, the brands in the best position to succeed in this more expensive environment were the largest brands with the biggest media budgets. Conversely, many smaller brands found they could no longer afford even the bare-bones schedule necessary to maintain a minimal year-round presence. Some were forced to abandon the networks completely and concentrate on secondary TV and print media.

THE ADVERTISING GAP

Reeling from the sticker shock of network prices, advertisers, both large and small, sought another form of relief. Since there was no way they could control network costs, many attempted to control their expenditures by shortening the length of their commercial messages. Historically the networks would accept no spot shorter than 30 seconds in length. But in 1983, bowing to advertiser pressure, they began to accept 15-second commercials as well as the standard 30-second spots.

Encouraged by early research that suggested 15s were 60 to 80 percent as effective as 30s, marketers steadily increased their use of these shorter units. But as 15s proliferated, another problem developed. The once pristine network environment became cluttered with shorter, more eclectic product messages. Once again, the brands best equipped to deal with commercial clutter were the largest brands with the biggest budgets.

COMMERCIAL CLUTTER

According to a study on 15-second television commercials published by the Association of National Advertisers, "Back in 1969, TV viewers saw only 2,000 commercials per week; by 1987, they were up to 5,600 commercials a week. . . . During an average week in 1989, 15-second commercials on network TV numbered 2,325, a 37.9 percent share of the total 6,132 commercials aired."[4]

In this cluttered environment, ANA researchers concluded that 15s could best be used to hammer home the names of well-known brands. At the same time, they believed 15s usually did not provide enough time to describe the advantages of one product versus another. Since superiority messages are necessary to gain share from category leaders, this placed smaller products at a severe disadvantage.

This disadvantage was further exacerbated by the network's decision to increase the ratio of commercial time to programming time. A study conducted by a consortium of advertising trade associations concluded, "All the networks have boosted non-program time over the past five years. CBS had the biggest increase, with 11 minutes and 40 seconds per hour of non-program material during prime time, up 13 percent from 1984."[5]

MEDIA FRAGMENTATION

In addition to the growing clutter on the networks, yet another problem faced marketers. While the cost of advertising time was on the rise, it seemed fewer people were actually tuning in! Due to the explosive growth of cable TV and VCRs, the networks' total share of the national viewing audience began to show serious declines. Since prices didn't decline proportionately, the medium grew even more expensive on a cost per thousand basis.

By 1990 cable TV had penetrated over 50 percent of all households. Depending on the cable system, cable subscribers were offered a dazzling array of 25 to 100 cable channels. In addition, by 1990 the incidence of VCR ownership had also risen to 50 percent of households. On any given evening, these consumers could chose to watch first-run movies or other forms of entertainment completely free of commercial messages.

Tempted by the availability of alternative video, the once solid network audience began to break apart. In an article entitled, "The Last Gasp of the Mass Media?" *Forbes* observed, "Back in 1978, ABC, NBC, and CBS had a lock on viewers, with 90 percent of the television audience during prime time. By last year [1989], that share had dropped to 67 percent."[6]

Like the other changes already described, the fragmentation of the network audience negatively impacted all marketers striving to reach mass targets. But once again, the brands with the biggest budgets were in a better position to compensate for the declines. By supplementing their network schedules with cable TV and other secondary media, these brands were able to maintain their advertising reach. Unable to afford the premiums associated with such media bundling, smaller products had to content themselves with eaching more limited target groups.

THE SALES PROMOTION GAP

While marketers were trying to deal with massive changes in advertising media, major shifts were in progress that were dramatically affecting their other key marketing tool—sales promotion. Consistent with trends developing elsewhere, these changes shifted the balance in favor of the biggest players with the deepest pockets.

Rising Promotion Spending

Historically marketers have tended to invest a larger proportion of their dollars in promotion than in advertising. During the 80s the traditional ratio grew even more lopsided. By 1989 promotional spending accounted for 66 percent of all marketing dollars. According to an analysis by Marketing and Media Decisions, total promotional expenditures reached $135 billion, up 9 percent from the previous year. By comparison, estimated media spending was $71 billion (up 5 percent from 1988).[7]

In addition, another $24 billion was being spent on trade allowances. Among other things, this massive spending underwrote literally billions of cents-off coupons, cash refund offers, premiums, sweepstakes, and free samples. In many mature product categories, as many as 40 percent of all purchases were made in connection with some special deal. Adrift in this vast sea of spending and activity, smaller brands once again found themselves at a competitive disadvantage.

To illustrate the point, let's examine the most popular type of consumer promotion, the cents-off coupon. According to the "Donnelly Annual Survey of Promotional Practices," manufacturers distributed over 75 billion cents-off coupons in 1989. Seventy-seven percent of these arrived via the free-standing inserts in Sunday newspapers. To effectively break through this coupon clutter, most marketers chose to run full-page, four-color offers.

Now let's apply some simple mathematics. The average media and printing cost of a four-color page is $500,000. The average face value of a consumer coupon is 50 cents. Assuming an average circulation of 35 million, a redemption rate of 2 percent, and a handling charge of 10 cents per unit, the total cost of the program comes to about $900,000. To compete successfully in many categories, manufacturers had to offer at least three such coupons per year. Yet again, the competitive advantages of scale are self-evident.

In a more extreme example, both Coke and Pepsi planned multimillion-dollar consumer contests in connection with the 1991 Super Bowl. The first prize in the Diet Coke game was $1 million. Pepsi countered with an interactive game in which consumers called a toll-free number that appeared in Diet Pepsi commercials before and during the game. To out-do the competition, the first *three* prizes offered were $1 million annuities.[8]

Problems at Retail

During the 1980s, smaller brands and new products alike started to feel the squeeze in the area of retail promotion. This pressure was the result of two primary factors:

1. The consolidation of supermarket and other mass distribution outlets in the hands of a few large competitors.

2. The trade's tendency to concentrate promotional activities behind a select group of fast-moving items.

During the past decade food stores, drug stores, and mass merchandisers—the three traditional distribution outlets for consumer products—were subject to the same economic forces affecting the entire retailing industry. Because of simple profit pressures and takeover activity, the number of key competitors in each class declined significantly during this period. As a result those retailers fortunate enough to have survived when the 90s began found themselves with greater clout than they had ever experienced before.

For example, the average supermarket today carries about 25,000 different products. In addition about 10,000 new items vie for shelf space each year. This intense competition for shelf space, coupled with the harsh reality that 80 to 90 percent of all new-product entries fail, gave birth to a new phenomenon known as the slotting allowance.

The Slotting Allowance

Simply stated, a slotting allowance is an incremental allowance paid to induce the trade to take on a new item. Clearly the slotting allowance raises the ante for all manufacturers. But unquestionably this additional business cost has the most impact on companies trying to introduce new brands or line-extend smaller franchises.

As expressed by a senior executive of a major East Coast supermarket chain, the rationale for the slotting allowance is that "manufacturers need to realize that a new item can cost a retailer about $3,000–5,000 just to take it in, when you consider the cost of paperwork, warehousing, and so forth. Then, if the product doesn't work, you have the additional cost of discontinuing it."[9]

The FTC has reviewed slotting allowances and ruled them to be completely legal. However, this new policy places heavy financial burdens on less-established marketers. According to a report in the *San Francisco Chronicle*, "For just a square foot or two of shelf space in a single store, the slotting allowance might top $100, although the one-time fee varies widely at different chains in different regions of the country. . . . [One] company with annual sales of $10 million spent $500,000 on slotting fees in just two markets—Los Angeles and New York."[10]

Another variation on this theme is the so-called failure fee now under consideration by some leading retailers. Under this scenario, manufacturers would have to pay a failure fee or penalty if a new product didn't sell an agreed-upon number of units within the initial six months. If enacted, this policy would further disadvantage marketers of new products and smaller brands looking to expand their franchise.

Failure fees and slotting allowances aren't the only obstacles confronting new products. In order to gain new distribution, manufacturers must also offer retailers high introductory allowances, then back up these programs with massive consumer couponing, sampling, and advertising campaigns. As a result, the total cost of introducing a new product has more than doubled in the past five years. Currently, it is estimated to be approximately $30 million.[11]

Focus on High-Turn Items

Another development that has limited the ability of new products and smaller brands to compete successfully is the trade's tendency to concentrate ongoing promotional support behind a few fast-moving products. In high-volume operations where profit margins are slim, velocity or turnover is the name of the game. To draw the greatest numbers of customers into their stores, mass retailers must feature brands with the largest consumer bases. These products are often featured as "loss leaders." In other words, they are priced below cost to attract customers into the stores. Once in, most customers will purchase other products at normal profit margins.

In such a discount environment, it is extremely difficult for new products and smaller brands to keep their heads above water. Even when manufacturers can convince the trade to promote such brands, these manufacturers can't afford to promote as often or as competitively as their larger counterparts. Drawn into a tit-for-tat situation, most new products and smaller brands will be overwhelmed by bigger brands with larger war chests.

The promotional problems of new or less-established products are underscored by the emergence in recent years of a new class of trade—the price warehouses. It is the stated policy of these high-volume, super-discount stores to carry only the two best-selling sizes of the top two or three category brands. In these outlets, it is literally impossible for lesser products to obtain even a single shelf facing. As price warehouses grow in popularity and draw business from more traditional outlets, the position of category leaders will be further solidified.

THE TECHNOLOGY GAP

In addition to the many advantages of size discussed so far, a new and qualitatively different advantage is now beginning to appear. Once firmly established, it has the potential to devastate smaller competitors. This advantage comes in the form of costly, yet cost-effective information technology. This new technology is allowing major retailers and manufacturers to monitor their business with a precision never before imagined.

From the retailers' perspective, computerized checkout scanners are providing the databases necessary to keep constant track of inventories and sales. Although up-front investments in equipment and software can be enormous, once in place this technology allows retailers to know exactly which products are selling or not selling. As an example, according to industry sources, Walmart now has access to complete daily sales information just 90 minutes after store closing.

As the precision of information technology continues to reshape retailing, there is simply no place to hide. If brands are not generating the level of weekly sales required to support their shelf space, they are scaled back or even eliminated. True to the old adage, knowledge is power. The knowledge provided by modern information technology is now allowing retailers to turn the tables on manufacturers, who have historically known more about product movement in stores than retailers have. Aided by computers, a direct correlation is now developing between trade support and actual levels of consumer purchases. In the process, the concept that "the big get bigger" is quickly becoming a self-fulfilling prophecy.

When it comes to information technology, advantages of size

aren't limited to retailers. Major manufacturers are aggressively pursuing technological advantages as well. Once again, it is checkout scanners that provide much of the basic information. *Business Week* described it this way in an article titled "How Software Is Making Food Sales a Piece of Cake":

> For over a decade, scanners at supermarket checkout counters have been collecting data about what products are being bought at what price. But at first software didn't exist to present the information in a form marketing management could easily use. . . .
>
> By the mid-1980s, A.C. Nielsen Co. and others had developed systems to sort out data by brand. Since then, though, "the amount of scanner information has increased something like 500-fold," says Danny L. Moore, Nielsen vice president for product development. . . .
>
> To manage this rising tide of data, Nielsen and software makers Information Resources and Metaphor Computer Systems have recently developed "quasi-expert" systems. These automatically break down brand performance within regions and detail how competing products are doing, which promotions work, and whether specific store displays are attracting customers. They also generate summary reports with graphs that highlight unusual product performance.[12]

In creating successful marketing programs, this kind of sales information can be invaluable. It is analogous to competing with your eyes wide open while your opponents are stumbling along blindfolded. But data like these do not come cheap. Depending on the level of detail required, annual costs for tracking just one brand can run into the millions. Unless heavily subsidized by their parent companies, most smaller brands can't afford an investment of this magnitude. Consequently, many slip farther behind in the management of their business.

Sensing a major competitive advantage, many large companies have now begun to design and implement their own proprietary information management systems. In most instances data purchased from outside suppliers is supplemented by internally generated data. Proprietary systems offer the additional benefit of consolidating data from a variety of sources into a single data base, then customizing the presentation of this information for use by individual departments and functional groups throughout the organization.

Today one of the most useful types of proprietary input is information from the field sales force. Ten years ago, sales reports were written manually by the individual salesperson. In many instances weeks or sometimes even months passed before this information found its way to the appropriate person in management empowered to act on the data. But just as checkout scanners revolutionized the way retailers manage information, another technological development, the hand-held computer, has forever altered sales force reporting techniques.

The snack food marketer Frito-Lay is an acknowledged leader in the application of electronic databases to sales and marketing programs. During the 1980s, the company invested over $40 million to purchase portable, hand-held computers for each of its 10,000 sales representatives. Utilizing these state-of-the-art devices, the company is able to update daily information on over 100 different product lines in more than 400,000 stores throughout the country.

According to a recent *New York Times* report,

> The small computers are used to track inventories at every retail store and to enter orders. The devices are also connected in delivery trucks to mini-printers that prepare invoices telling the sales representatives which items are to be restocked at each stop on their route, as well as the prices and promotional discounts if any.
>
> At the end of the day, the hand-held computer is connected to an IBM minicomputer at a Frito-Lay distribution center so that results can be sent to headquarters. Afterward, the central computer sends to the hand-held computers information on switches in pricing and promotions for use the next day.[13]

MICROMARKETING

Former House Speaker Tip O'Neill once observed, "All politics are local." The same observation could just as easily have been made about marketing. Over the past few years, a new term— *micromarketing*—has entered the industry vernacular. The term describes the custom-tailoring of national programs to local situations. Advanced electronic information systems such as Frito-Lay's allow managers to micro-market with remarkable efficiency. While less-sophisticated competitors are still executing one-size-fits-all national programs across local markets, Frito-Lay's data system helps the company develop customized programs to take advantage of varying local conditions.

Beyond the enhanced capabilities that exist today, micro-marketers expect their abilities to increase substantially in the near future. According to the *New York Times*,

> Frito-Lay plans next to add data about sales and advertising expenses to the sales support system. But many local marketers are looking forward more to next year's introduction of what Frito-Lay calls the trade development system. The program will help account executives to spot situations where store owners can increase profits by displaying more Frito-Lay products.
>
> It will also analyze sales data for more than 200 grocery products of all types to develop suggested layouts. Tests suggest that presentations to store managers, which sales representatives traditionally labored over for 10 days or more, can be run off the computer in 15 minutes, said Charles Feld, head of Frito-Lay's information systems.[14]

As this software is perfected, the technology gap between companies like Frito-Lay and its competitors will widen further.

FUTURE SHOCK

In addition to the forces described in this chapter that are polarizing consumer markets and increasing the gaps between large and small brands, another overarching condition of contemporary life greatly favors large, established products. Author Alvin Toffler first identified this condition in the late 60s and dubbed it *future shock*. In a nutshell, future shock is a state of psychological inertia that develops when individuals are confronted with more change than they can deal with effectively.

Since accelerating change is now a fact of life, it follows that the incidence of future shock is on the rise in contemporary society. In an effort to cope with accelerating rates of change, many people cling to the tried and true in every aspect of their lives, be it politics, religion, or purchase behavior. In marketing, *tried and true* translates into established, familiar products.

One of the primary characteristics of future shock is information overload. Information increases in direct proportion to change. In some cases the information itself is the change. While computerization is helping science and industry cope with tidal waves of new data, individuals are largely left to fend for themselves. For most Americans the challenge to make sense of things begins with the endless stream of commercial and noncommercial information appearing on their TV screens.

Today's viewers are being bombarded by far more commercial messages than they are capable of processing. For example, during the 10-year period from 1979 to 1989, the average number of commercials per week on network television alone increased 57 percent from 3,937 to 6,169.[15] According to some estimates, contemporary consumers have been exposed to more than 1 million commercial messages by the time they reach 40.[16] To protect themselves from this advertising onslaught, consumers' attention spans are shrinking dramatically.

Recently the Roper research organization polled about 2,000 Americans to measure their general response to TV commercials. Their findings weren't encouraging to advertisers, especially those attempting to introduce new products or increase awareness and trial of smaller brands. The study reported that the most pervasive response to the start of any commercial is "to get annoyed" (58 percent). The next four most common reactions were: "get up; do something else" (45%); "talk to others" (42%); "get amused by commercial" (33%); and "switch channel" (28%).[17]

In recent years the "switch channel" response has been encouraged by the availability of remote control tuners, which give the viewer the magical power to "zap" away annoying commercials without stirring from the comfortable couch. As ownership of tuners continues to rise, the zapping phenomenon is destined to increase. The introduction of TVs that allow consumers to view several channels simultaneously through electronic windows is also contributing to this behavior.

While TV is the primary source of commercial information overload, fragmentation of the print medium is also contributing to the general noise level in most consumers' lives. Over the past decade hundreds of new publications have been introduced to reach specialty subgroups. Add to this the proliferation of new media, such as advertising on shopping carts and videocassettes, and it is no wonder consumers' brains are beginning to shut down. The information age has now resulted in overload for most Americans.

RETREAT TO PRIVACY

But the commercial media are not the only areas of vital interest to marketers that are falling victim to future shock. Market research—the manufacturer's primary feedback link with its customer base—is also experiencing severe setbacks. Today, because of a decrease in leisure time and an increase in everyday stress, growing numbers of consumers are simply unwilling to participate in market research studies. This problem was the subject of a recent *New York Times* report.

According to the article,

> Market researchers are discovering that if you ask a simple question these days, you might not get any answers at all. Deluged by a growing number of telephone solicitations and increasingly jealous of their time, more and more Americans are refusing to participate in market research surveys. . . . That leaves researchers confronting a new question: Is the ever-shrinking segment of consumers who will talk to them really representative of the rest of the population? . . .[18]

> A study by Walker Research, a St. Louis company that tracks trends in the market research industry, found in 1988 that 34 percent of all adults contacted said they had refused an interview request during the previous year, up from 15 percent in the company's 1982 survey. Members of the Council of American Survey Research Organizations, an industry association, reported that 38 percent of consumers turned down interviews in 1988.

The primary causes of this decline are privacy concerns and inconvenience. Increasingly consumers are reluctant to provide personal information to an anonymous voice at the other end of the phone. But even those willing to participate often find they don't have the time to get involved when researchers call at the dinner hour or at the end of a long day.

THE TIME CRUNCH

Ultimately the rising time pressures created by future shock may have the most insidious impact on the aspirations of consumer product marketers. As accelerating change makes everyday life more complex, consumers have less time to devote to every aspect of their lives—family, work, and shopping. Caught in a never-ending time crunch, they seek to simplify their purchase decisions by sticking to known products. So it seems that even the pace of life itself is conspiring against the growth of less-established products.

In a recent study *Progressive Grocer* magazine concluded that the average shopper spends less than 12 seconds in a product area before making a decision, while 42 percent spend five seconds or less.[19] As harried consumers race through supermarkets and other retail outlets, there is little time for comparison shopping. When purchase decisions are almost instantaneous, force of habit usually prevails.

Not long ago an article called "Americans 'Paralyzed' by Choices" appeared in a major newspaper. The author observed that

an increasing number of sociologists and other experts are beginning to believe that the marketplace may have outsmarted itself. Americans, they say, are becoming overwhelmed, even paralyzed, by all these choices, and some experts say that the apathy is spilling over into other areas of daily life.

"Choices do not make life easier; they make it more difficult, for all of us," said Dr. David A. Goslin, president of the American Institute for Research in Washington. . . . Many people cope with the variety by focusing on what is familiar.[20]

During the 1980s in the political realm, people focused on the familiar by reelecting incumbents at a higher rate than at any other time in our history. As the 80s wore on, it became increasingly difficult to dislodge an incumbent president, senator, or any elected official. In the marketing realm the same tendency was evident. There was a widening psychological gap in consumers' minds between small brands and large, established brands. To the many advantages of size was added yet another: Whether selling a president or a product, incumbency—defined as a recognized position of leadership—became an obstacle that proved to be difficult for most challengers to surmount.

As the 80s came to a close, it was beginning to seem that all the elements were teaming up against smaller brands. The various economies of scale had come together to create a powerful surge of marketing momentum behind large brands. If the surge continued to grow in strength, it appeared destined to sweep away any obstacles in its path.

NOTES

1. "The Last Gasp of the Mass Media," *Forbes*, September 17, 1990, p. 176.
2. "Fox TV Ad Sales Stun Competition," *San Francisco Chronicle*, July 4, 1990, p. E-6.
3. Michael Lev, "Super Bowl 25," *The New York Times*, January 6, 1991, p. C-5.
4. "Improved Marketing Productivity or Advertising's Vietnam?" *A.N.A. Advertising Research Committee Report*, July 3, 1990, p. 3.
5. "Commercial Clutter," *San Francisco Chronicle*, July 2, 1990, p. C-3.
6. "The Last Gasp of the Mass Media," *Forbes*, September 17, 1990, p. 176.
7. Russ Bowman, "Sales Promotion," *Marketing & Media Decisions*, July 1990, p. 20.
8. Kim Foltz, "Coke and Pepsi Square Off in the Super Bowl of Colas," *New York Times*, January 7, 1991, p. C-10.
9. Bruce Fox, "Scan Data Gives Retailers Upper Hand," *Supermarket News*, November 16, 1987, p. 1.
10. Jamie Beckett, "How Supermarkets Sell Shelf Space," *San Francisco Chronicle*, September 13, 1990, p. 1.
11. Eben Shapiro, *New Products Clog Grocery Stores*," *New York Times*, May 29, 1990, p. C-1.
12. "How Software Is Making Food Sales a Piece of Cake," *Business Week*, July 2, 1990, p. 55.
13. Barnaby J. Feder, "Frito-Lay's Speedy Data Network," *New York Times*, November 8, 1990, p. C-1.

14. Ibid.
15. "Improved Marketing Productivity or Advertising's Vietnam?" A.N.A. Advertising Research Committee Report, July 3, 1990, p. 3.
16. Deborah Baldwin, "Read This," *Common Cause Magazine*, May/June, 1991, p. 30.
17. "TV Turnoff," Corridor Talk, *Adweek*, July 2, 1990.
18. Randall Rothenberg, "Surveys Proliferate, But Answers Dwindle," *New York Times*, October 5, 1990, p. A-1.
19. Warren Thayer, "Do Your Customers Know What's on Special? Do They Care?" *Progressive Grocer*, May 1990, p. 81.
20. Lena Williams, "Americans 'Paralyzed' by Choices," *San Francisco Chronicle*, February 14, 1990, p. 1.

Chapter Three

A New Approach to Marketing

If large brands are destined to be at center stage in the marketing playhouse for the foreseeable future, the question becomes, How do you distinguish a large brand from a megabrand—a star from a superstar?

Sheer size is certainly a distinguishing characteristic, and in Chapter 2 the advantages of size were discussed across a range of manufacturing and marketing activities. Breadth of product line is another. In Chapter 1 the concept of share maximization through line extension was introduced as today's key growth strategy.

But these two characteristics alone don't adequately describe a megabrand. Not every large, extended line of products is a megabrand or fated to become one. If a brand is to rise to megabrand status, a third ingredient must be present in the mix. This critical ingredient is the marketing process itself.

In the world around us, nothing is static. In a state of constant flux, it's the ongoing process of marketing which creates, maintains, and helps to define a megabrand. The marketing process is why some once-dominant brands today command only a fraction of their former market shares. The marketing process is also why a few of America's leading trademarks have successfully evolved into overarching corporate entities.

Bringing all of these key characteristics together into a single definition,

A megabrand is a dominant line of products, built around an established base brand, that offers consumers variations of a core product benefit and is marketed in a consistent and complementary manner.

Now, let's examine each of the individual elements in this definition in greater detail.

DOMINANCE

Within any product category, it is easy to identify the leaders simply on the basis of market share. But correctly selecting the dominant brand from the full lineup of leaders is a more difficult proposition. Precisely when does a brand become dominant? How is this dominance quantified? What are its benefits?

In a paper titled "The Battle for Brand Dominance," Larry Light, president of the Arcature Corporation, proposes one of the most precise definitions of market dominance. While it may not be applicable to every category situation, it is quite insightful and worth considering in some detail. He begins his discussion by describing the financial rewards of being among the select group of category leaders.

An examination of the return on investment (pre-interest, pre-tax) versus market rank for 2,746 businesses in the PIMS database shows that there is a clear relationship between market rank and profitability. Here is the evidence:

Market Rank versus Return on Investment

Rank	ROI
1	31
2	21
	47
3	16
4+	12

Businesses with a market rank of 1 average an ROI of 31 percent. Those with a rank of 4 or worse deliver an ROI of only 12 percent.

Market leaders are about two and a half times more profitable as those businesses which rank 4 + .

Light then goes on to draw the critical distinction between a market leader and a market dominator.

We recognize, however, that all leaders are not the same. There are dominators and there are marginal leaders. A market "dominator" is defined as a business with sales volume at least 1.5 times its nearest competitor. The remainder of number 1 businesses are defined as marginal leaders:

Market Rank versus ROI

Rank	ROI
Leaders	
Dominator	34
Marginal Leader	26
Competitors	
Competitor 2	21
Competitor 3	16
Followers	12

Market rank is a critical determinant of business performance. A market dominator is 52 percent more profitable than its nearest competitor (Competitor 2) and is an amazing 183 percent more profitable than the market followers. The desire for market leadership and domination makes good business sense. Leadership is profitable. Domination is most profitable.[1]

Light's precise definition of market dominance is probably not directly translatable to all category situations. For example, it seems reasonable to say that two products, Coke and Pepsi, dominate the soft-drink market. Likewise, two brands, Crest and Colgate, enjoy dominant positions in the toothpaste business. Nonetheless the distinction he draws between a market leader (a product with a significant market share) and a market dominator (one with a controlling market share) is a critical point that distinguishes a large brand from a true megabrand.

LINE OF PRODUCTS

In today's fragmented markets no single product can appeal to a wide enough group of consumers to maintain a broad-based franchise. In order to attract and hold sophisticated consumers, a brand must offer a variety of choices within its line.

When Procter & Gamble introduced Crest in 1955, there was a single formula available in three sizes. Today there are six different formulas in 44 different shapes and sizes. For 67 years Lysol existed as a single product in a plain, brown bottle. At last count the Lysol line included six different products that come in more than 25 different sizes. The Vaseline line contained only one product, petroleum jelly, for 100 years. Now there are seven distinct line extensions available in 80 different shapes and sizes.

As discussed earlier, line extension is the most basic building block of megabrand marketing and the key to share maximization.

BUILT AROUND AN ESTABLISHED BASE BRAND

Before there can be a house, there must be a foundation. Before there can be a megabrand, there must be a solid and stable base brand. Line extensions literally build on the equity that the base brand has established with consumers. As a result they draw the majority of their users from the base franchise.

To line-extend effectively, the base brand must have achieved critical mass in terms of absolute sales; that is, its sales volume must be large enough to sustain itself and also pass along users to the new item. If the base brand's volume has not achieved this critical size, or if its sales volume is not properly maintained, two often interrelated problems can occur:

1. **The group of switchers to the new line extension won't be adequate to sustain the new entry.** In this instance, consumer take-away will never rise to the level necessary to maintain shelf space and the product will fail.

2. **The line extension will so dilute base-brand sales that the base business will begin to lose distribution on its slower-moving sizes.** This occurrence exposes the base brand to inroads by competitive products.

As a product line grows, its base business may evolve from a single product to a group of high-volume line extensions. Nonetheless the same principles hold true. Each component of the base business must be large enough to sustain itself, while at the same time serving as the primary source of volume for new additions. Proper management of the base-brand business is fundamental to line extension success.

One of the classic mistakes in marketing is to extend a line prematurely. In this instance manufacturers will introduce a series of line extensions in quick succession before the base is strong enough to support them. The result: the entire line is weakened and destabilized. What starts out looking like the road to easy, incremental profits turns out being the path to serious financial losses.

VARIATIONS OF CORE PRODUCT BENEFIT

In addition to being firmly established in absolute size, the base brand must also be established in category positioning. In a broad sense the brand must enjoy high levels of consumer awareness. Ideally it should be one of a small set of products that consumers instantly call to mind whenever the category is mentioned.

Beyond this linkage with a general product category, there should also be an immediate association of the brand with a specific product benefit. For example, market research shows that most consumers recall Tylenol not only as a pain reliever, but as the analgesic which provides "safe" pain relief. Similarly consumers identify Tide not just as a detergent, but as the detergent that gets out "tough dirt." This strong association with a particular benefit represents the psychological foundation for subsequent line extension.

Once the core product benefit is firmly established, new brand extensions can proceed to offer consumers variations of this basic theme. For example, Extra Strength Tylenol can provide "safe" pain relief in an extra-strength dosage, while Children's Tylenol delivers this same safe pain-relief benefit in a children's formula. In the detergent category, liquid Tide can offer the same effectiveness as Tide powder but with greater ease of use for consumers who like to pour detergent directly on to tough dirt or stains.

On the other hand, if a product's core benefit has not been well defined, consumers will find additional line extensions confusing and be unlikely to try them. It is not surprising that consumers didn't flock to Extra Strength Datril when this line extension was introduced in the late 1970s. Since Bristol-Myers had not been able to establish the base, regular-strength product or clearly communicate its aspirin-free benefit, the entire analgesic line eventually failed, at great expense to the company.

MARKETED IN A CONSISTENT AND COMPLEMENTARY MANNER

The advantages of marketing synergy are central to the entire megabrand concept. Unlike new-product development where companies must start from scratch and "reinvent the wheel," line extensions of an established brand can ride on the coattails of the base product. They can and *should* take full advantage of the marketing momentum built through years of promotion, advertising, and sales efforts.

To maximize the marketing efficiencies inherent in the megabrand approach, managers must take great pains to market each line item in a consistent and complementary manner. This consistency and cohesiveness must pertain to the abstract concerns of managing the brand's image across a variety of products, as well as to the concrete details of individual marketing programs. If handled properly, the efficiencies across products can be considerable; if handled haphazardly, the outcome can be counterproductive and potentially damaging.

Consistent Brand Image

To begin with, the extended brand line must present a consistent face or image to consumers. This doesn't mean that the image of each product must be exactly the same. However, it does mean that each product must share a common family character. Image or character is most often expressed in the particular traits or qualities that consumers strongly associate with a given brand name.

If, for example, wholesomeness is a fundamental component of the Campbell's soup image, then wholesomeness should be reinforced in every piece of marketing communications. To focus on trendiness (e.g., new flavors) at the expense of wholesomeness would be inconsistent with Campbell's well-established image and, over time, could muddy the brand's profile.

In years past, brand image was created largely through words. For this reason it was important that advertising campaigns include a theme line that captured the essence of the brand positioning and image. Campbell's accomplished this objective very effectively with its famous theme, "That's what Campbell's soups are . . . mmm, mmm, good!"

In today's video environment, brand image is created primarily through the use of visual symbols. Therefore, consistency of visual imagery is imperative. In addition to their verbal theme, "Soup is good food," Campbell's commercials always portray images of wholesome kids enjoying a hearty bowl of soup in a comfortable, family setting. Over time, consumers have come to associate such visual images with Campbell's. As a result Campbell's spots instantly communicate and reinforce Campbell's brand image.

Complementary Marketing Programs

When correctly managed, an extended line offers a company the means for maintaining a continuous high profile with consumers and the trade alike. When created in a thoughtful manner, a megabrand marketing program can have a collective impact far greater than the sum of its parts. But achieving this cumulative impact requires careful planning and coordination across the entire product line. Without a central, unifying vision, the various products and programs in the mix can often work at cross-purposes.

There is certainly no one "correct" approach to achieving the desired integration. In a very real sense there is infinite potential for creativity and innovation. However, several underlying principles should always be observed:

Principle #1: Individual products within a megabrand line should never compete for consumer or trade attention. Promotions, advertising, and other marketing activities should be scheduled to showcase specific products. No one should ever be put in a situation where an either-or decision forces the selection of one line product at the expense of another.

Principle #2: Wherever possible, products should be bundled together in programs that are beneficial to all the participants. This practice allows the line to achieve maximum synergy and impact. For example, many larger marketers commonly engage in theme promotions in which consumers can obtain a premium or qualify for sweepstakes entry by submitting proofs of purchase from a number of products within the line.

Principle #3: Marketing activities for individual products should be chronologically staggered whenever possible. By executing programs in sequence, rather than simultaneously, significant line activity can be maintained on a continuing basis throughout the year.

In Chapter 6 the achievement of maximum marketing synergy through the planning and coordination of line activities will be discussed in greater detail.

CHALLENGING THE CONVENTIONAL WISDOM

As evident from the discussion above, aggressive, coordinated line extension is the essence of the megabrand. This concept stands in sharp contrast to the conservative marketing principles utilized by leading consumer product companies during the rapid growth era of the 50s and 60s. In the past such companies viewed line extensions as defensive in nature. In other words they were introduced to prevent users from switching to competitive products.

Today many savvy marketers recognize the offensive capabilities of line extensions to significantly increase their overall business. But, as always, perception lags behind reality. Old attitudes persist that distort vision and limit the potential for success. Yet when the precepts of the conventional wisdom are juxtaposed against the realities of the new wisdom, it's difficult to continue to embrace the old, time-worn beliefs.

In the discussion that follows, the conventional wisdom, which warns against aggressive line extension, will be compared to the new, emerging wisdom, which is pro–line extension. In particular, four key dimensions will be examined:

1. Impact on brand image.
2. Effect on customer base.
3. Implications for marketing spending.
4. Opportunities in related categories.

IMPACT ON BRAND IMAGE

Historically one of the most serious criticisms against aggressive line extension has been that it has a corrosive, negative effect on brand image. According to this conventional point of view, numerous line extensions dilute a brand's image, thereby weakening its market position and making it vulnerable to competitive attack.

While this viewpoint may have had some validity in the past, it no longer stands the test of empirical evaluation. In truth the brands with the strongest images in today's fragmented marketplace have been aggressive line extenders. This position is corroborated by the findings in a national survey on America's most popular brands conducted by the Landor Associates consulting group.

According to the 1989 survey results,[2] the 10 U.S. brands held in the highest esteem are:

1. Campbell's
2. Disney
3. Black & Decker
4. Kodak
5. Coca-Cola
6. Hershey's
7. Kellogg's
8. Johnson & Johnson
9. Hallmark
10. Levi's

If the conventional wisdom against aggressive line extension were true, we would expect to find that brands such as these with the strongest images have been extremely conservative on the line-extension front. In fact the exact opposite is true. Let's focus for a moment on Campbell's—the number one consumer product brand and the number one brand overall in the Landor study.

Line Proliferation

By the company's own count, five major lines of soup products are currently marketed under the Campbell's brand name (e.g., Campbell's Red, Campbell's Classics, etc.). Two of these lines have been introduced over the past decade. Among these lines there is a total of 55 different flavor varieties. In recent years the company has also extended its brand name to related product categories, such as frozen, microwaveable lunch products. In light of Campbell's extreme popularity in the Landor survey, all of this activity appears to have done nothing to diminish Campbell's brand image.

And what about Coca-Cola, the second most popular consumer product and the fifth most popular brand overall? On American supermarket shelves today there are four major Coke lines: Coke, Coke Classic, Diet Coke, and Cherry Coke. Each of these is sold in a regular and caffeine-free variety. Today, there are eight different kinds of Coke where not long ago there was just one. Once again based on the Landor results, this proliferation of line extensions doesn't appear to have hurt the brand's consumer image.

The fact is that not only Campbell's and Coke, but each of the brands on Landor's most-respected list have followed a strategy of aggressive line extension. The results from this major, ongoing brand image study strongly support the new wisdom that line extensions are key to maintaining a clear, positive brand image. In addition the findings suggest that

Line extensions work to strengthen a brand's image by keeping it fresh and contemporary.

In today's rapidly changing marketplace, static product lines can quickly develop an old-fashioned image, while a properly extended line can keep its image forever young.

EFFECT ON CUSTOMER BASE

The second conventional lament about aggressive line extensions is that they are inherently cannibalistic. In other words they don't expand the customer base but simply shift users from product to product. Further line extensions erode brand loyalty by encouraging a pattern of switching among a brand's own users. According to this logic, if consumers get into the habit of switching within the line, at some point they will be more likely to move outside the line altogether and switch to a competitive product.

Impact of Cannibalization

As discussed earlier, marketers must be mindful not to extend a brand with an insufficient base. However, assuming adequate sales volume, the conventional criticism again ignores contemporary reality. Even if the cannibalization rate were 100 percent (which is rarely the case), line extensions would still make good economic sense.

The logic is straightforward. Since line extensions are innovations, they should be priced at a premium versus the preexisting line. When this is the case, even assuming 100 percent brand switching (cannibalization), total dollar sales for the line will increase as users trade up to the more expensive product. If pricing for the new line extension has been correctly set to cover incremental product costs, absolute line profit will also rise.

Brand Switching

The traditional argument against cannibalization is a red herring in another respect. In today's fragmented marketplace, brand switching has become a way of life. In order to maintain a broad-based franchise, a brand must offer its customers a variety of choices within its line. If it doesn't, it's inevitable that competition will offer these choices outside the line. As such, having options available today doesn't erode brand loyalty, it reinforces it.

Potential for Incremental Sales

Ultimately the key to growth in a world of multiple choices lies in identifying and introducing new alternatives in advance of the competition. When line extensions are introduced before similar, competitive entries, they become more than merely cannibalistic; they become offensive, business-building propositions.

Depending on the degree of innovation, experience has shown that even mature packaged goods brands can add up to 5 percent in incremental sales with a single, well-conceived item. Seventy-five-year-old Clorox recently accomplished just such a feat with its Lemon Scent line extension. So did venerable, old Tide with its innovative Tide with Bleach product.

Today every leading consumer product line is significantly larger than it was 10 years ago. It's no accident that in most cases market share has increased too. By taking an offensive approach to line extension, proactive brands have been able to expand their business base, while those products that have chosen to react defensively have been locked in a negative, downward spiral. In the final analysis, line extensions aren't an option for contemporary brands seeking to maintain a broad franchise. They are a necessity.

IMPLICATIONS FOR MARKETING SPENDING

In the past a prevailing opinion among many marketers was that line extensions required little in the way of separate, ongoing advertising or promotional support. According to the conventional wisdom, separate advertising, focusing specifically on the new line extension, was called for only during the introductory phase (usually the initial six months). After that the line extension could be supported indirectly through base-brand advertising. Often this involved the use of line extension "tags" at the end of base-brand commercials.

Likewise in the promotional arena, the conventional thinking was that separate, trial-oriented activities were necessary only during a brief, introductory period. Once completed, the line extension's promotions could be folded into the base brand's program. The fact that line extensions could be kept afloat "efficiently" with minimal advertising and promotional support was seen as one of their few advantages.

In today's markets this conventional minimalist approach to line extension support has come under serious challenge. Without question, there still are circumstances where this tactic is appropriate—often in situations where the new items represent only minor innovations, such as new flavors or scents. But when the innovations are major, line extensions are often supported via separate advertising and promotions well beyond the launch period. Sometimes this support continues indefinitely.

Ongoing Support

The decision to provide a line extension with major, ongoing marketing support is directly linked to the ability of the product to attract new users into a franchise. This ability is, in turn, related to the importance of the benefit variation the line extension provides. If consumers perceive the benefit variation to be important, then trial within and outside the franchise can be high.

However, trial of an important line extension first requires awareness. In order to maximize awareness, specific advertising must be continued for at least 18 to 24 months. By the same token trial-generating promotional programs such as sampling and high-value couponing must be extended. To curtail this support any sooner would unnecessarily limit the product's business-building potential.

Support Benefit Variation

Even after trial has topped out, an important benefit variation provides the basis for separate marketing support. Many companies now make the strategic decision that they can most effectively defend and maintain a major line extension by continuing to reinforce its benefit variation via stand-alone advertising and promotion. Separate support keeps a line extension's image fresh and distinct. It also makes it more difficult for competitors to make inroads.

For example, Procter & Gamble still runs a special campaign for Crest Tartar Control Formula in addition to basic Crest copy. Clearly the distinct benefit variation that this product delivers has drawn large numbers of new users into the Crest fold and P&G is not about to expose these new customers to competitive assault.

Today many of America's most successful product lines simultaneously support a number of items with individual advertising campaigns and aggressive, item-specific promotional programs. At the same time these competitors still reap substantial spending efficiencies. It is important to note that these efficiencies are primarily a function of absolute size and market leadership, not the elimination of line support. In fact, in most cases, total line spending steadily increases. Contrary to the conventional wisdom, line-extension sales and profit are not always maximized by passively riding the gravy train pulled by a large base brand.

OPPORTUNITIES IN RELATED CATEGORIES

Possibly the strongest warning voiced by conventional thinkers regarding aggressive line extension pertains to the transference of established brand names into related but different categories. According to the old guard, this should never be done under any circumstances.

The traditionalists believe that the fundamental strength of a brand name lies in its category roots. If these roots are cut by transplanting the brand into another category, the product will be doomed to wither in inhospitable soil. Additionally the original product line will be damaged and its future growth stunted. It's much better to enter a new category with a new brand and a new brand name.

In earlier times the wisdom of this thinking seemed self-evident and was rarely challenged. But as costs of new-brand introductions skyrocketed to prohibitive heights, harsh realities forced marketers to cautiously poke at these sacrosanct assumptions. What they discovered was that category extension was a difficult but not impossible task. The challenge lay in precisely defining and exploiting a brand's equity with consumers.

Using techniques that will be described in greater detail in the next chapter, marketers began to move into these largely uncharted waters. More often than not, these forays involved redefining category boundaries in a way that expanded a brand's competitive arena. For example, Planters successfully accomplished this maneuver when it transferred its trademark from the nut category to the broader category of snacks. Jell-O did likewise, using Pudding Pops to push out its category walls from packaged desserts to frozen confectioneries.

Sometimes these leaps have been more dramatic. These efforts have been based on out-of-the-box thinking that redefines a brand's core benefit in a way that transcends a number of otherwise distinct categories. For example, Arm & Hammer utilized such an approach when it redefined the benefits of baking soda to include freshening. Making use of this tactic, the company not only extended the use of the base brand (with the baking-soda-in-the-refrigerator campaign) but set the stage for a later successful move into the home cleaning category with its Rug and Carpet Cleaner product.

Obviously this type of category extension involves a much greater degree of risk. A more recent Arm & Hammer entry into the oral hygiene market—Arm & Hammer toothpaste—seems to be meeting with a much cooler consumer reception. At this point its ultimate success is unclear. Such questionable results may be a function of an inherent benefit conflict between something you put in your mouth and something you put on your floor. In this instance Arm & Hammer may have strayed too far from its core benefit roots.

As we move into the 1990s, the conventional prohibition against category extension is falling by the wayside, along with other classic criticisms of line extension. Increasingly, major companies are engaging in more line-extension activity. Over time, continuous, successful category extension can result in the evolution of a brand trademark into a corporate trademark. However, this process is extremely difficult, requiring an exceptionally strong brand name and a particularly malleable core benefit. In light of the many complications, reincarnation as a corporate entity is not likely to be the ultimate destiny of most megabrands.

Over the past decade the emergence of megabrands has forced managers to rethink and abandon many old assumptions and adopt a dramatic, new approach to marketing. As the 90s unfold, one final tenet of the conventional wisdom may still fall before the onslaught of the megabrands—the concept of product life cycle.

According to this theory, products (like human beings) have a preordained life cycle that moves through birth, maturity, and decline. However with megabrands, the life cycle may be much lengthier than previously thought. By ongoing innovation and line extension, a megabrand is constantly renewing itself in the marketplace. Through this process of rejuvenation, it may be possible to prolong the life cycle of a megabrand, perhaps indefinitely.

Even if the megabrands turn out to be just as mortal as others, it is certain that they are likely to be among the long-term survivors in the competitive jungle. Today there may be five or six large category competitors—including one megabrand; tomorrow there may be only three. In a very real sense contemporary marketers are engaged in a high stakes game of musical chairs. When the music stops, there will not be enough seats to go around.

In the next part the principles of megabrand management will be discussed in greater detail in an effort to guide managers of major product lines through the challenging times ahead. For those responsible for the management of smaller products, there will be follow-up discussion of the principles of niche marketing—a proven, alternative marketing approach that can help smaller products survive and prosper in a world of larger products.

For managers of all brands, regardless of size, there is no question that the rules of the marketing game are rapidly changing. New attitudes, approaches, and skills will be required to succeed in these new circumstances. As always, those who are first to adopt these new attitudes, master these new skills, and put them to work in the marketplace will achieve important, competitive advantages that are likely to endure for years to come.

NOTES

1. Larry Light, "The Battle for Brand Dominance," presentation to the Advertising Research Foundation 35th Annual Conference, New York, April 1989, p. 128.
2. Jamie Beckett, "Americans Give U.S. Brands Top Ratings," *San Francisco Chronicle*, September 13, 1990, p. C-1.

PART 2

THE PRINCIPLES OF MEGABRAND MANAGEMENT

Chapter Four

Expanding Brand Positioning

Many years ago the famous French novelist Balzac observed,"A man's character is his fate." In the world of marketing, the same might be said of a brand's positioning. To a very large extent, a brand's positioning is its fate. Positioning exerts a powerful, lasting influence that literally determines the course of a product's life.

In essence brand positioning is a master strategy. Not only does it clearly identify a brand's location in the market, it also provides the foundation for all subsequent marketing activities. Every aspect of the marketing program—objectives, strategies, and tactics—flows from brand positioning. It is the most fundamental strategic decision that can be made about a product.

IMPORTANCE OF BROAD POSITIONING

Precise positioning is critically important for all brands, but for megabrands the stakes are even higher. By virtue of its scope and breadth, a megabrand's positioning is distinct from that of other products. In building a megabrand, it is absolutely essential to construct a positioning broad enough to support an extended product line and thus appeal to a wide range of consumers. To accomplish this, there must be an underlying, functional linkage among all the line items that can be clearly perceived and understood.

Without this underlying linkage a megabrand will not have the strategic integrity to support its many line extensions. In the presence of seemingly unrelated entries, a cognitive dissonance will be created in the minds of consumers and the brand structure will start to break apart. Consumers will reject the association of the line extensions with the base product, and the psychological bonds that hold the line together will begin to disintegrate.

For example, consumers have come to expect all Excedrin products to be extra-strength. If Excedrin suddenly introduced a regular-strength product, it would create a high level of consumer confusion that would, in turn, begin to undermine the brand's positioning. Likewise, if Windex were to suddenly introduce a wood-cleaning product after years of selling glass cleaner, consumer confusion would ensue and, again, the brand's established positioning would begin to erode.

Like Excedrin and Windex, the positionings of most major brands in the marketplace today are narrow. The reasons for this are a function of the market conditions that existed at the time of the brand introductions. Most of these products were launched in the post–World War II era when market segmentation was the order of the day. To differentiate these brands from competitors, they were consciously positioned by the manufacturers to appeal to narrow market segments. As a result their infrastructures were not designed to support the heavy weights of broad product lines.

REVERSING THE TREND

But with the economic changes of the 80s and the coming of the megabrands, the pendulum began to swing back in the opposite direction. Today as opportunities shift away from new product introductions to extensions of existing product lines, marketers of large brands are no longer seeking to reinforce product positionings within narrow market segments. Instead they are attempting to expand these positionings and maximize appeal across entire categories.

This major shift in strategy has been made possible by the flexibility that line extensions provide. No longer does a single product have to appeal to every consumer. Now line extensions can be developed that appeal to specific subsets within a broader user group. By custom-tailoring benefit packages for individual market segments, line extensions can dramatically extend a brand's appeal.

SYSTEMATIC APPROACH

However, before line extensions can be successfully introduced, consumers must be conceptually ready to receive them. In other words the consumer's mind-set about the product and its place in the market must be expansive enough to comfortably include these new line items. Some brands—principally older products introduced in the era before market segmentation—were "born" with broad positionings capable of sustaining extensive line extensions. However, the majority of contemporary brands do not fall into this category.

It is true that the process of line-extending itself, when conducted over a prolonged period, can expand a brand's positioning. As line extensions are introduced, their presence and advertising messages begin to alter and enlarge consumers' perceptions of the line's positioning in the marketplace. But to evolve a brand's positioning in this hit or miss manner is risky business with high potential for failure. It's far wiser to systematically build a line according to predetermined strategic guidelines provided by an expanded brand positioning.

In today's competitive environment where rapid line extension is the key to growth, new products must be introduced quickly and frequently. To ensure the acceptance of these new products by consumers, brand positionings must be expanded through a conscious, systematic process. This process of expanding brand positioning will be discussed in detail in the following section.

The discussion will begin with a comprehensive review of the key components of brand positioning that are the basic building blocks in any expansion activity. It will also include an extensive review of advertising and marketing communications techniques.

Unlike a person, a brand cannot speak for itself. In fact a brand's positioning is so inextricably linked to its communications program that it can have no real existence apart from it. In essence the medium truly *is* the message.

BRAND POSITIONING DEFINED

In human terms a brand's positioning could be described as its basic identity. It is the image or picture that consumers have in their minds about a particular product that distinguishes it from all other brands. A brand's positioning tells consumers how a product fits into their everyday lives and how it should be used. It provides the mental coordinates that allow consumers to precisely locate a product within a dizzying array of choices.

Because of its importance in the marketing process, corporations have worked very hard over the years to develop a concise definition of brand positioning. While the exact wording may vary somewhat, most definitions would be likely to say:

Brand positioning is the way a company wants consumers to think about a product.

To make this description more relevant to the everyday world, packaged goods marketers, such as Kraft/General Foods, have broken down the concept of product positioning into three component parts:

1. Market target.
2. Frame of reference.
3. Point of difference.

Simply stated,

The market target is the group of consumers most likely to be potential users of a brand.

The frame of reference refers to the set of products that a brand competes with.

The point of difference is the particular benefit that consumers identify with a product.

To illustrate how these components work, let us consider a few brief examples. Using this format, the positioning for Secret antiperspirant might be expressed as follows:

For women concerned about perspiration wetness (1), Secret is the one brand of antiperspirant (2) that is strong enough for a man, but gentle enough for a woman (3).

In the mouthwash category, the positioning for Listerine could be described as:

For adults concerned about oral hygiene (1), Listerine is the one brand of mouthwash (2) that not only stops bad breath but also helps prevent gum disease (3).

In the cough/cold category, the positioning for Nyquil cold medicine could be stated as:

For adult cold sufferers (1), Nyquil is the one brand of cold remedy (2) that effectively prevents cold symptoms at night so one can sleep (3).

While it may seem rather simple, developing a succinct positioning statement often requires weeks of analysis and group discussion. As this occurs, serious debate often takes place over each component of the positioning statement. However, once agreed upon and committed to writing, the positioning statement will keep a marketing program squarely on track. It will also help managers avoid countless wrong turns and prevent the squandering of valuable resources.

In considering the three-part positioning statement described above, it is clear that the various statement components are interrelated. Each one directly affects the others. While all three components are important, the keystone of any product positioning is the point of difference. The point of difference ultimately determines both the target audience and competitive set. As the most critical factor, it is appropriate to consider this component in greater detail.

POINT OF DIFFERENCE AS KEY COMPONENT

While the point of difference is rooted in the attributes of the product, it is often distinct from these attributes. The point of difference is always expressed as a consumer end-benefit that the product delivers more effectively than other alternatives.

Most products have more than one point of difference from competitive brands. As a result, managers must determine through market research the point of difference that provides the maximum consumer leverage and is consistent with actual product performance. In other words they must identify the benefit with the strongest appeal across the broadest target group.

As our understanding of human behavior becomes more sophisticated, it is apparent that a product's consumer benefit has two interconnected parts. Both parts are so distinctive that it is appropriate to consider them as two separate benefits—the rational and the emotional. As contemporary marketers attempt to differentiate brands with few functional differences, emotional benefits take on increased importance.

PRODUCT BENEFITS

All human beings experience the world through the twin filters of reason and emotion. Since we are both thinking and feeling creatures, all our decisions, including purchase decisions, are motivated by both rational and emotional forces. For this reason the product benefit, or point of differentiation, that drives brand positioning must be understood and expressed in both rational and emotional terms. In an age of parity products and commodity markets, the powerful expression of a brand's emotional benefit is often the only means of effectively distinguishing it from other products.

While all products deliver both rational and emotional benefits, both benefits are rarely of equal importance in the purchase decision. Depending on the nature of the product, the relative value of the rational and emotional benefits will fluctuate dramatically. Some purchase decisions are highly emotional, while others are very rational and pragmatic. Understanding the relationship between a brand's emotional and rational benefits is absolutely critical to effective positioning.

Over the past 15 years, Dick Vaughn, corporate director of research and planning for Foote, Cone & Belding Communications, has made a careful study of the rational and emotional components in consumer purchase behavior. One of the important byproducts of his work is a conceptual tool known as the FCB grid. The grid is a dual-axis matrix that helps marketers properly position and advertise their products.

The horizontal axis of the FCB grid is labeled "Think-Feel." This axis measures the extent to which a brand purchase decision is driven primarily by rational or emotional considerations. The grid's vertical axis is tagged "High Involvement/Low Involvement." This axis plots the degree to which consumers are personally invested in the particular purchase activity.

Using data gathered from over 20,000 consumer interviews about more than 500 different products, Vaughn has been able to plot a broad range of purchase decisions. For example, consider two product extremes: detergent and perfume. While laundry detergent falls into the lower left quadrant represented by "low think/low involvement," expensive perfume falls into the upper right-hand quadrant—"high feel/high involvement." By using the FCB grid or similar techniques, marketers today have the ability to measure the relative importance of rational versus emotional benefits in the proper positioning of a product.[1]

Understanding the Rational Benefit

As the term implies, the rational benefit is the functional, utilitarian advantage that a brand provides the consumer. It is the practical reason for buying a product. In the traditional product positioning statement, the rational benefit is expressed in straightforward, logical language. For example, Clorox bleach "gets out stains detergents leave behind," or Crest "prevents cavities."

When translated to the medium of consumer advertising, the rational benefit is communicated in a very logical manner. Probably the most effective approach to advertising rational product benefits is the concept of unique selling proposition (USP) developed during the 1950s by Rosser Reeves—one of the legends of the advertising industry. A USP was a succinct advertising theme line designed to communicate in a catchy, memorable way the logical reason why a consumer should purchase a particular product.

During the 1950s and 1960s the USP was the hallmark of every campaign produced by Reeves's agency, Ted Bates & Co., including such advertising classics as "M&M's melt in your mouth, not in your hand," and "Anacin relieves the pain of tension headache." Typically the USP was accompanied by support points that provided rational "proof" of the benefit claim and a product demonstration that provided additional, visual evidence of product performance.

Since seeing is believing on television, visual demonstration has always been an important component of many advertising campaigns. From animated drawings to side-by-side comparisons and scientific graphs, visual demonstrations are particularly convincing in our contemporary video society. In fact there appears to be a growing trend towards building entire commercials around memorable visual demonstration.

Understanding the Emotional Benefit

As meaningful performance differences among products continue to dissipate, marketers have focused on preempting emotional benefits as a means of creating product differentiation. As they become more familiar with this area, they are discovering that nonrational appeals can be far more powerful and persuasive than previously suspected. Once considered a secondary add-on, the emotional end-benefit is now recognized as a key component of contemporary product positioning.

In a major speech to the Advertising Research Foundation, Josh McQueen, director of marketing research for the Leo Burnett Company, talked about the role of emotion in modern-day product marketing. According to McQueen,

> Emotion is important to brand choice because attitudes toward a brand are based upon both how it functions and how it feels, and both contribute to persuasion. When there are no meaningful functional differences between brands in a category, the brand choice

balance shifts to "How will it feel?" When a brand delivers a major functional difference, the right emotional benefit will help enhance brand perceptions.[2]

A similar sentiment has been voiced by Foote, Cone & Belding's research director, Dick Vaughn. In a recent agency paper, Vaughn stated,

> As they [consumers] move from satisfying basically utilitarian to more expressive needs, they increasingly begin to look for products and services that both "perform" right and "feel" right. In brief, consumers seek appeals to both head and heart that address the fullness of themselves as people. . . .
>
> Leading marketers who want to hold or get consumers must direct their advertising and promotional energies toward rational *and* emotional communications that work together for total effect. A Unique Selling Proposition is no longer strategically sufficient; a USF—Unique Selling Feeling—must be added whenever and wherever it can give a brand a much-needed edge.[3]

Link to Product Experience

Like the rational product benefit, selection of the appropriate emotional benefit is not arbitrary. The emotional benefit must have an inherent relationship to the product itself. As such, the relationship does not grow out of a concrete product attribute; rather, it flows out of the consumer's experience of the product and it fits in that person's life.

For example, on a rational, functional level, a consumer may use Pledge furniture polish because it makes furniture shine. On an emotional level, this same consumer may be using Pledge to protect family heirlooms that have great sentimental value. When defining a brand's emotional benefit, the challenge is to identify the single emotional button with the greatest relevance and importance.

Identifying and successfully communicating a brand's emotional benefit requires a diametrically different approach from doing the same for its rational benefit. Although consumers may be strongly influenced by their feelings about a brand, they may often have great difficulty describing these feelings to others. While emotions can be articulated through language, they are experienced most profoundly on a nonverbal, often preconscious level. The communication of emotion to others is accomplished most forcefully through channels such as facial expression and voice pitch than by language alone.

For years marketers had to identify a brand's emotional benefit largely on the basis of their own instincts and intuitions. But a few rudimentary techniques did exist that could assist them in this process. One of the most popular of these techniques was simple personification. Using personification, a researcher would ask consumers, "If this brand were a person, what kind of person would it be?" Invariably, answers included such responses as weak or strong, harsh or gentle, caring or cold, and so on.

The personification technique is still in widespread use today. However, because it is language-based, it often cannot provide the deep, psychological insights necessary to directly tap into a brand's emotional core. To break through this communication barrier, nonverbal approaches are required. Recently, new techniques originally developed by psychologists and behavioral scientists have been applied to the problem with considerable success.

NONVERBAL RESEARCH TECHNIQUES

According to some researchers, up to 90 percent of the information processed by human beings comes in visual form. Therefore it is not surprising that many new, nonverbal techniques are vision- or image-based. They can be as complex as state-of-the art biofeedback devices or as primitive as simple line drawings. A recent *Wall Street Journal* article described how the line drawing approach was employed to solve a creative problem for American Express.

> The McCann-Erickson ad agency resorted to stick-figure sketches in research on its American Express Gold Card account. Focus group interviews hadn't made clear consumers' differing perceptions of gold card and green card holders.
>
> The drawings, however, were much more illuminating. In one set, for example, the gold card user was portrayed as a broad-shouldered man standing in an active position, while the green

card user was a "couch potato" in front of a TV set. Based on such pictures and other research, the agency decided to market the gold card as a "symbol of responsibility for people who have control over their lives."[4]

The advertising agency Foote, Cone & Belding has taken nonverbal advertising research far beyond the line drawing stage. During the 1980s the agency invested significant time and money in the development of a number of proprietary visual techniques designed to pinpoint emotional responses to brands. One of these techniques which has been used successfully throughout the agency is called Image Configurations (ICON).

ICON utilizes a library of 60 photos of scenic situations that have been defined in terms of emotional content. During an ICON exercise, consumers are asked to associate the photos with specific brands. By linking the pictures with the brands, marketers can identify their brand's emotional associations and benefits compared to other products in the category.

EMOTION IN ADVERTISING

Years ago an unknown marketing pundit made the profound observation that "TV is a visual medium." While the truth of this statement is clearly evident, it is remarkable how often marketers lose sight of this reality and become obsessed with the language of commercials. In TV advertising the vast majority of product information is communicated through video bites. This is particularly true when communicating emotional benefits.

For example, the marketers of Extra Strength Tylenol made a major strategic breakthrough when they first articulated the brand's emotional benefit as trust. They made an equally critical breakthrough when they chose to communicate this benefit through consumer testimonials. Because testimonials involve real people, not actors, they carry with them added credibility. It is hard to imagine a more appropriate context in which to deliver a message of product trust.

In the Tylenol testimonials, the image of the real person on screen conveys believability—even before the speaker utters a word. Of course Johnson & Johnson (J&J) added several important embellishments to their testimonials for Extra Strength Tylenol that made them even more persuasive. For example, the Tylenol users appeared to be cast for their honest, wholesome looks. In addition they were always filmed against the backdrop of their own homes. This visually reinforced the message of trust and authenticity.

More recently the Thompson Medical Company broke a new ad campaign for its Slim-Fast reducing line. According to the advertising executive responsible for the account, the objective of the campaign was to sell both the product's rational and emotional benefits. The commercials focused on a group of well-proportioned people having a good time at the beach, playing games, and exercising. The executive explained, "We wanted to underscore the message that Slim-Fast stands for weight loss tied to good health and feeling good . . . . The ads demonstrate that Slim-Fast isn't just a fad, it's part of a way of life."[5]

Today J&J, Thompson Medical, and other sophisticated advertisers recognize the tremendous power of television to communicate emotions at a subtle, almost subconscious level. As the baby boom generation weaned on TV enters mid-life, mass marketers are relying increasingly on the visual image, not the spoken word, to sell their products and services.

MUSIC AND EMOTION

Physiologically another sense can communicate emotion on an even more basic level than sight—sound. For years advertisers have been using music in their radio and TV commercials to enhance the communication of emotional end-benefits. This has been particularly true in categories like soft drinks and beers, where products are purchased primarily for emotional gratification, not functional purposes. As awareness of the persuasive power of sound continues to increase, music is finding increasing application even in categories where there are also strong rational benefits.

In a recent interview, media theorist Tony Schwartz philosophized about the power of sight and sound in broadcast advertising. According to Schwartz,

Broadcasting, unlike print, is not a perceived medium but a received medium. Because people must be taught to read, they learn to consciously analyze the written word. But they interpret sounds and visual images naturally and instantaneously, beginning at birth, making it easier for a communicator to affect the public with sights and sounds that evoke people's existing subconscious beliefs and desires.[6]

One category where music has recently been introduced with great success is laundry products. Traditionally laundry-product advertising has been fairly straightforward, replete with rational arguments and before-and-after product demonstrations. But in 1986 Clorox introduced a new campaign for its color-safe bleach brand, Clorox-2, that was a radical departure from previous category efforts. The new campaign contained little of the standard laundry product fare. Rather, the commercials were built around a piece of music entitled, "Momma's Got the Magic of Clorox-2."

The commercials featured vignettes of romping children in brightly colored clothing. The jingle lyrics proclaimed, "Momma makes yellow, yellow like a dandelion. Momma makes white, white like the sunshine. Momma makes blue twinkle like her eyes do. Momma's got the magic of Clorox-2." The emotional message conveyed was the pride a mother feels making her children's clothes look as beautiful as possible.

The consumer response was outstanding. By communicating the emotional end-benefit through the use of music, Clorox-2 was able to build upon and enhance the appeal of its rational product story. In addition, music was so successful for Clorox-2 that it eventually became a connecting element in all Clorox bleach brand advertising. While the jingles varied from one campaign to the next, the emotional communication of pride in the family's appearance was consistent across all the brand's advertising.

One positive outcome of communicating emotional end-benefits through music or other techniques is that consumers tend to like these commercials better. As research has shown, this is more important than had previously been thought. As discussed in a *Wall Street Journal* article,

> Until recently, advertising scholars found no evidence that liking a commercial had anything to do with its effectiveness, and there

was even a school of thought suggesting that ads people hated could be quite effective.

But a recent study by the Advertising Research Foundation in New York concluded that likability was the single best determinant of whether a commercial would be successful. And the Ogilvy Center for Research and Development separately found that people were twice as likely to change their brand preference if they liked a commercial.[7]

EXPANDING BRAND POSITIONING

Having discussed the rational and emotional components of a brand's benefit and how these benefits are conveyed through advertising, it is time to return to the subject of expanding brand positioning. As previously mentioned, the positionings of most major brands today are somewhat narrow. In order to support extended product lines, these positionings must be expanded. This expanded positioning can be accomplished by redefining the brand's benefits (point of difference) to appeal to a broader target group. In the process the competitive set and the target audience are also enlarged.

Given the growing diversity of the consumer base, it would be impossible for any single product to successfully appeal to today's many constituencies. Therefore line extensions are a critical factor in efforts to expand base-brand positioning. Enhanced positionings are only made possible by the ability of line extensions to export the core benefit of the base brand to different segments and categories. Line extensions customize a core benefit to meet specific segment and category needs.

Expanding the Rational Benefit

Expanding the rational benefit is the semantic equivalent of finding the least common denominator. The process involves taking the brand's rational benefit, which is usually developed to fit a specific market segment, and reducing it to a more general statement that has relevance to a broader base of consumers. It is important to note that *relevance* is the operative word here. If the rational benefit statement becomes too diluted, it will become irrelevant and nonmotivating. In such a situation the positioning of the total line will be undermined.

Graphically, expanding the rational benefit is akin to pushing out the circumference of a circle while maintaining its center or focal point. As an example let us consider the Tylenol brand. For years Johnson & Johnson positioned the brand as a safe analgesic. Using the circle analogy, this positioning was like a circle with "safety" as its focal point and its circumference defined as "headache relief." (See Figure 4–1.)

In the mid-70s J&J began to expand this positioning by rethinking the brand's rational benefit. First the definition of the brand's headache benefit was expanded to include all dosage strengths (e.g., extra strength, children's strength, etc.). Then in the 1980s the rational benefit was broadened again, from headache relief to cough/cold allergy relief and to relief of other conditions. In the process J&J was careful to maintain Tylenol's underlying safety orientation. In graphic terms the circumference of the circle was expanded to include additional nonprescription drug categories, while keeping safety as the focal point.

Having successfully positioned Tylenol within this expanded competitive circle, J&J has been able to enlarge Tylenol's competitive frame of reference beyond the $3 billion analgesic category to include other portions of the $12 billion over-the-counter drug business. In so doing, the company has redefined Tylenol's target

FIGURE 4–1
Expanding the Rational Benefit

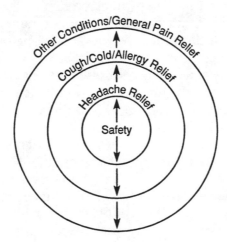

audience to include large new groups of potential users. Building on this enhanced positioning, J&J has already introduced a successful line of cold remedies under the general heading of Tylenol Cold, as well as a Tylenol Sinus line for sinus sufferers. Based upon these events and the success that J&J has had to date, it is likely that Tylenol will continue to enter additional drug categories in the future.

Ultimately the only limitation on J&J's ability to enhance the Tylenol brand positioning will be the physical limitations of the product itself. Tylenol's safety benefit is linked to a product attribute—the pain-relieving ingredient acetaminophen, a key ingredient in all Tylenol formulas. For some nonprescription drug products such as stomach remedies, acetaminophen pain relief is not appropriate. For this reason it is unlikely that Tylenol will ever be a major factor in this business or others like it.

Enhancing the Emotional Benefit

To build an extended megabrand line, it is also necessary to enhance the core emotional benefit of the base brand. To do so, marketers must shape the consumer's perception of the emotional benefit so that it can be easily carried over to products in different segments and categories. The process for accomplishing this enhancement is the antithesis of its rational counterpart—just as reason can be seen as the antithesis of emotion. While megabrand marketers must express their brand's rational benefit in the most expansive terms, they must communicate the emotional benefit in a distilled, intense, and poignant manner.

Intensity of feeling must be heightened before an emotional benefit can be successfully transferred across segments and categories. Unlike logic, which is precise, emotions can be amorphous and vague. To make the emotional benefit shine more brightly, it must have a sharp, directed focus. To illustrate this point, let us return to the Tylenol example.

Since its introduction Tylenol's rational benefit—safe pain relief—has had as its counterpoint the emotional benefit of confidence and security. At first the emotional benefit lacked a sharp focus. Early efforts were designed to leverage the strong emotional impact of physician endorsement with claims such as "More doctors recommend Tylenol than all aspirin brands combined." As time went on, however, J&J turned up the level of emotional intensity.

In TV and print advertising, doctor endorsement gave way to more powerful emotional endorsements from hospitals—the institutions charged with the preservation of life itself. Product claims shifted to "Hospitals recommend Tylenol 10 to 1 over all aspirin brands." Eventually Tylenol's emotional benefit reached an even higher level of intensity when the company chose to identify it with the basic feeling of trust. At this point the claim evolved to the simple but emotionally charged statement, "Hospitals trust Tylenol."

The process of emotional enhancement can be depicted graphically as reducing the circumference of a circle to more closely circumscribe its focal point. The illustration that follows shows how Johnson & Johnson successfully enhanced the Tylenol emotional benefit from everyday confidence to solid, unshakeable trust. (See Figure 4–2.)

Just as a high-voltage transmitter allows a radio signal to travel thousands of miles, an intense emotional benefit can be more readily transferred across a range of products. A more generalized benefit becomes diffuse and breaks up the farther it travels from its source. However, the method of communication is all-important. Advertising, particularly TV advertising, is more than a vehicle. It is part of the enhancement process itself. In fact the enhancement of an emotional benefit is inseparable from its expression.

After identifying the testimonial as the ideal commercial format for communicating the trust benefit, J&J proceeded to utilize this approach for many Tylenol line extensions. Today commercials for Co-Tylenol cold medicine and Tylenol allergy medicine also employ user testimonials. These campaigns portray before-and-after situations where sufferers are cured of their conditions on camera. With respect to visuals and language, they are evocative of the Extra-Strength Tylenol spots. They work on their own, as well as in conjunction with advertising for other Tylenol products, to communicate the trust benefit on an underlying emotional level.

FIGURE 4–2
Enhancing the Emotional Benefit

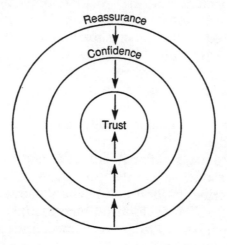

BRAND CHARACTER

When the rational and emotional benefits of a brand's positioning have been effectively communicated over time, a brand character emerges that is often bigger than the sum of its many parts. A brand's character is rooted in the basic benefits of the product itself but is also more than these benefits and distinct from them. In psychological terms it is the persona or face that a product presents to the world at large. However, since a product clearly has no life of its own, a brand's character is created consciously and deliberately by its managers through advertising and other marketing communications.

Advertising executives Larry Chiagouris and Leslie Perrell had this to say about the creation of brand character through advertising:

> The main premise of brand character is that advertising must not only communicate what the brand is or what it does, but must also communicate a sense of who the brand is, how it looks and feels, and what its role is in the consumer's life. Exploring these new dimensions of a product and communicating them through adver-

tising helps to distinguish it from other products, just like an individual's personality distinguishes that person from any other.[8]

Brand Symbols

Sometimes the multifaceted aspects of brand character actually coalesce in the form of a concrete personality, like the Pillsbury Doughboy, the Green Giant, or the Keebler Elves. Such personalities can be the embodiment of an enhanced product positioning. Once created, they tend to be ubiquitous, appearing in every commercial, print ad, and packaging panel for every product in the line. In effect, brand symbols are the living, physical incarnation of the brand's rational and emotional benefits.

Because consumers perceive these brand symbols in much the same manner as they perceive real people, they often relate to them as if they were human. Over the years they develop familiar, emotional relationships with these animated brand characters. Such "personal" relationships are a marketer's fantasy, since they provide an instantaneous, warm connection with the brand and any new product in the line.

Unquestionably the most popular new brand character to emerge in recent years wasn't a single character at all but an entire group. When the California Raisin Advisory Board's Dancing Raisins appeared on the scene in 1986, they became an overnight sensation. They quickly transformed the image of raisins from a dull fruit into a healthy, "with it" snack food. In the process they expanded raisins' product positioning from a small segment of the fruit category into the large and fast-growing snack food business.

In this chapter we have discussed expanding brand positioning—an essential first step in building a megabrand line. An expanded brand positioning defines the parameters of line development and forges the strategic links that bind the line together in the marketplace. While there are systematic ways to approach this challenge, expanding brand positioning will always remain just as much an art as a science. Success requires a special combination of analysis and imagination. In the end developing an expanded product positioning and communicating it persuasively to consumers is essentially a creative act. What will ultimately separate the winning companies from the rest of the pack—the megabrands from the other brands—are not the systems that can be used by all, but the degree of innovation brought to the task.

NOTES

1. Foote, Cone & Belding Communications, Inc., "A Guide to the FCB Grid," 1987.
2. Josh McQueen, "A Definition of Emotion and the Importance of Subtlety," Sixth Annual ARF Copy Research Workshop, May 22, 1989, p.122.
3. Foote, Cone & Belding Communications, Inc., "Worldwide Creative Excellence and the Importance of Nonverbal Advertising Research, An Agency Viewpoint," April 15, 1988, p. 1.
4. Ronald Alsop, "Advertisers Put Consumers on the Couch . . . Research Probes Emotional Ties to Products," *The Wall Street Journal*, May 13, 1988, p. 19.
5. Kim Foltz, "Slim-Fast to Sell Itself as a 'Way of Life,'" *The New York Times*, December 31, 1990.
6. Randall Rothenberg,"A Legend Turns to Selling Social Change to Companies," *New York Times*, January 14, 1991, p. C-8.
7. Michael J. McCarthy, "Mind Probe," Marketing in the '90s, *The Wall Street Journal*, March 22, 1991, p. B3.
8. Larry Chiagouris and Leslie Perrell, "Asking the Right Questions," *Review of Business*, Summer 1989, p. 5.

Chapter Five
Developing the Line

Like an architect's blueprint, a megabrand's positioning provides the conceptual framework for developing the product line. But as grand as this vision might be, without the appropriate line extensions, the brand's potential will never be realized.

Building from an expanded positioning, a megabrand has the potential to compete successfully in every segment of its "host" category. By developing customized line items to fit each category segment, a megabrand can capture its share of existing category business. But to realize its full volume potential, a megabrand must do more than simply reflect the present category configuration. It must actually *reshape and redefine* the category through innovative entries.

In a very real sense a megabrand is a microcosm of its own category. The structure of its line reflects the structure of its category, the dynamics of its growth parallel the dynamics of the category, and innovations in the category are quickly mirrored in the megabrand array. Conversely the category at large will rapidly duplicate any significant innovations created by the megabrand.

Developing an expanded megabrand line is a complex, ongoing task. When approached in an ad hoc, opportunistic manner, there are countless opportunities for wrong turns, wasted effort, and squandered resources. However, when approached in a planned, organized manner, the job can be accomplished effectively and efficiently. This chapter provides a systematic approach for megabrand line development that limits risks and maximizes opportunity.

The approach is a five-step process:

1. Setting the priorities.
2. Identifying the opportunities.
3. Developing the products.
4. Evaluating the upside.
5. Refilling the pipeline.

By utilizing this approach, managers should be better able to meet the ongoing demand for innovative line extensions today and in the future.

STEP 1: SETTING THE PRIORITIES

Within most marketing organizations at any point in time, numerous new product alternatives are competing for development dollars. As a result, marketers must be skillful in selecting the concepts with the greatest volume potential from the available options. When confronted with many options, experienced marketers usually follow a deductive approach. They start with the obvious and work backwards.

Ultimately any brand seeking to become a megabrand must take an aggressive approach to line extension. More often than not, it must be the first in its category to identify emerging marketplace opportunities and the first to introduce new products to take advantage of those opportunities, thereby preempting its competitors. However, before a brand can assume this proactive position, it must first secure its business base by protecting it from competitive threat.

Fill Competitive Gaps

As a general operating principle, a major brand must have an entry in every established market segment in order to secure its business from competitive attack. Therefore, the number one product development priority for a major brand line must be to fill any competitive "holes" that exist in its current product lineup. A failure to close these gaps or to respond quickly to a successful competitive innovation will inevitably weaken a brand's market position and expose it to a steady erosion of its user base.

In addition, by failing to respond in kind to a competitive entry, a brand risks the acceleration or snowballing of user loss over time. This snowballing effect can occur because one significant innovation often leads directly to another. If a brand has not matched the first advance, it will usually experience even more difficulty matching the second. Like a tiring distance runner, it will continue to fall farther behind until it is eventually lapped by the front-runner.

In matching a competitive product innovation, it is not necessary to develop a product with a superior performance profile. However, it *is* necessary to create products that perform at parity with the products already on the market. A brand's goal in this situation is to keep its users in the franchise by offering equivalent performance to competitive brands, not to attract new users by leapfrogging the competition with a second-generation product.

Most major brands today understand the importance of maintaining a complete product line and few have glaring competitive gaps. However, there are some instances where a particular brand's heritage is so closely linked to a specific market niche that it has never extended its line beyond that area. When confronted with this situation, brand management must make a difficult choice—content themselves with the niche position and ignore growth opportunities in the larger market or risk the protection of the existing niche by attempting to move the brand beyond it.

Recently Lever Brothers faced this dilemma with its Wisk detergent brand. Unlike most detergent products, Wisk was introduced in a liquid, not a powder form. For years Lever effectively leveraged the advantages of this form difference via a "pour directly on tough stains" strategy, communicated via its memorable, if somewhat abrasive, "ring around the collar" campaign. However, this message and advertising approach limited the brand to participation in only one segment of the detergent market.

As the competition within the liquid arena intensified, Lever decided to extend the Wisk franchise into the powder segment with the introduction of Wisk Powder in 1990. By launching Wisk powder, Lever management took a big gamble. By moving the brand away from its traditional roots and placing it in unfamiliar ground, they did increase the product's potential for growth; but they also raised the odds for failure. To date, the powder form has met with limited success and its long-term impact on the liquid franchise is still uncertain.

As long as a brand is responding to competitive developments, it is caught in a reactive position—always striving to minimize losses. To begin to grow toward megabrand status, a brand must at some point break out of this defensive mode and take an aggressive approach to line extension. To do this effectively, marketing managers must have the ability to systematically identify the opportunities, create prototype concepts and products, and evaluate their appeal. They must also have the personal and financial support of top management to back a proactive product-development program.

STEP 2: IDENTIFYING THE OPPORTUNITIES

In the ongoing struggle to identify product development opportunities, it is critical for marketers to remember that

Successful new products are consumer-driven, not technology-driven.

During the past 10 years there have been numerous examples of companies, enthralled by a new technology, that rushed products to market. In many cases these businesses discovered too late that consumers simply were not interested in their technology-driven ideas.

The marketing axiom, "Stay close to the consumer," is particularly critical to the successful development of new line extensions. Unfortunately, obeying this axiom is seldom as simple as it sounds. It is not enough for marketers to stay close to the customer. When in close proximity, they must also know what to listen for. While it's true that successful new products are consumer-driven, it's misleading to believe that they will be consumer-created. Even with the benefit of extensive consumer research, the hard work of creating new items still rests with marketers themselves.

How many thousands of brand managers have sat expec-
tantly behind two-way mirrors at focus group sessions, hoping
for a breakthrough idea? How many have come away disappointed when participants did not hand them the hoped-for innovation on a silver platter? Waiting for innovative ideas to emerge
from focus groups is akin to waiting for Santa Claus. For in today's mature markets, most of the obvious product improvements have already been made. While consumers can recognize a
good idea when they see one, it is unlikely that they will identify
and articulate one out of the clear blue sky!

Sources of Ideas

Today identifying opportunities for new-product development is
one of the most challenging and rewarding aspects of marketing
management. It is an assignment that requires a mixture of marketing art and science, both intuition and logic. While research
and analysis can help identify the most promising areas, in the
end it is simple, old-fashioned imagination that conceives the actual product concepts.

In the search for new-product opportunities, three underlying consumer currents can consistently inspire or stimulate new
product ideas. These three currents include:

1. Demographic trends.
2. Changes in consumer life-style.
3. Shifting consumer attitudes.

Of the three, demographic trends are the most easily quantified
and analyzed.

Demographic Trends

**Demographics can be defined as changes in population—its size,
age, structure, composition, employment, educational status, and
income.**

Of all these demographic measurements, possibly the most
significant today is age. In his book, *Innovation and Entrepreneurship*, management consultant Peter Drucker had this to say about
age:

Analysis of demographic changes begins with population figures. But absolute population is the least significant number. Age distribution is far more important . . . .

Particularly important in age distribution—and with the highest predictive value—are changes in the center of population gravity; that is, the age group which at any given time constitutes both the largest and the fastest-growing age cohort in the population.[1]

In modern times no demographic phenomenon has had greater impact or received closer scrutiny than the post–World War II baby boom. Included in the baby boom generation are 77 million Americans born between the years 1946 and 1964. They account for 31 percent of all U.S. citizens. As this age cohort moves through the population like a "pig through a python," the center of population gravity continues to shift. Each movement sets off chain reactions of new-product development.

As children who enjoyed playing and getting dirty, the baby boomers spawned many innovations in the laundry products category. As teenagers concerned with appearance, they stimulated the development of countless shampoos and hair-care products. As young adults striving to maintain their youthful figures, they inspired hundreds of diet foods, drinks, and reducing aids.

Today the baby boomers are entering mid-life. This latest demographic trend—the graying of America—suggests an enormous new array of product development opportunities. For megabrand marketers it offers the chance to further solidify the position of market dominance. By aggressively developing new line extensions that specifically address the needs of aging baby boomers, a megabrand should be able to maintain and expand its user base. The possibilities for new line extensions that appeal to mid-life Americans are limitless and stretch across all product categories. But certain businesses, such as foods and health and beauty aids, are particularly well positioned to take advantage of this important trend.

Other Demographic Factors

In addition to age, three other demographic factors merit discussion from a product development perspective. These are sex, marital status, and income. In the case of sex, while the overall ratio of men to women is not subject to dramatic shifts, the number of women with full-time jobs outside the home has increased dramatically during the past two decades. According to 1990 figures, 60 percent of U.S. women now fall into this category.

Working full-time places tremendous pressure on most women—many of whom also play the roles of housekeeper and primary parent. To marketers, these pressures create opportunities to develop more convenient product forms, thereby attracting large numbers of working women into their franchise. Three categories in an excellent position to capitalize on this demographic trend are food, household cleaning products, and child care items.

In recent years marketers have been looking more closely at marital status and have identified single Americans as an important prospect group. Today, singles are being targeted by a variety of product marketers from toothpastes to financial services. According to a recent report,

> The 1990 census shows about 23 million Americans live by themselves, a 91 percent jump for women since 1970 and a 156 percent increase for men over the same period . . . . But the market is even larger than these numbers suggest. Some 18 million adults aged 18 to 34 live with their parents or in college dormitories and have plenty of spending money. Throw in these other singles and the group has an estimated earning power of $660 billion.[2]

Finally the 1990 census figures revealed some significant changes in consumer income distribution. In particular the statistics show an increasing concentration of wealth among the top 20 percent of U.S. wage earners. Clearly this is not a positive development for society as a whole. However, income polarization does suggest that opportunities exist for more expensive premium items in many product lines. The development of high-end, gourmet food and beverage items is an example of new-product opportunity that is at least partially stimulated by income trends. On the opposite end, income polarization also suggests that opportunities exist for new "economy" items as well.

Changes in Consumer Life-Style
Until the early 70s, *life-style* was a term heard more often at country clubs than at marketing presentations. Then a little-known

market researcher, Daniel Yankelovich, published the first *Yankelovich Monitor*. Suddenly life-style was transformed into a subject worthy of serious study by consumer products companies.

The *Yankelovich Monitor* was the first large-scale national study of consumer attitudes and life-styles. According to *American Demographics*, "Life-style research was made possible by the advent of computers, which allowed large numbers of survey questions to be cross-tabulated easily. By combining statistical methods with psychological and sociological theories, psychographics provided a quantitative way to look at the qualities of consumers."[3]

Since the time of its initial publication, predictions in the *Monitor* have been followed closely by many major corporations. The *Monitor* was the first to identify the Yuppie (young, upwardly mobile urban professional), the Dinc (dual-income couple), and the now-infamous couch potato. Awareness of these life-style trends have helped marketers identify new areas for product development and more finely tune their marketing communications.

One aspect of life-style trends reported in the *Monitor* and elsewhere is the growing impact of technology on modern life. For example, 80 percent of American homes now own microwave ovens. The microwave phenomenon has created tremendous line extension opportunities for megabrand marketers in the food industry. By being the first to offer a wider variety of products in microwaveable packages, marketers have been able to attract microwave users from other product lines that did not offer a similar range of entree selections.

Shifting Consumer Attitudes

The third current that can generate opportunities for new-product development is shifting consumer attitudes. Major shifts in consumer attitudes often take years to gain momentum. But once under way, they can have a massive impact on consumer behavior. Two attitude shifts affecting the market today are growing concerns for personal health and concerns for the welfare of the environment. Both of these changing attitudes are creating opportunities for aggressive line extensions.

Growing health consciousness is manifesting itself most clearly in the food and beverage business. Foods and ingredients thought to be beneficial to good health are quickly finding their way into many new line items. Witness the abundance of new bran cereals. Conversely, ingredients that receive negative medical publicity stimulate their own "reactionary" line extensions. Consider the current assortment of caffeine-free sodas and teas, low-sodium frozen entrees, and low-cholesterol desserts.

Another category strongly affected by rising health consciousness is the health and beauty aids business. For example, as a result of growing consumer awareness of the dangers of excessive sun exposure, most skin-care lines now offer line extensions that include sunscreens. On the oral hygiene front, major toothpaste brands are meeting the emerging needs of the aging adult population by launching plaque-fighting line extensions to capitalize on growing consumer awareness of gum disease.

Environmental Concerns

In addition to increased concerns about personal health, today there is a widespread concern about our deteriorating environment. This consumer anxiety is creating both the necessity and the opportunity for reformulations and new line extensions. Cutting across all categories is the need for biodegradable packaging. There are also numerous occasions for new formulations in a variety of categories that can render products more "body safe" or "user friendly."

In a 1990 marketing supplement, *Adweek* observed,

> The last two years have seen a pronounced increase in new or reformulated products designed for green (pro-environment) positioning. By some reckonings, 5 percent of new product launches this year were for green products and the percentage is expected to grow.
>
> "If they continue to arrive at the present rate, new green products will account for 10 percent or more of total introductions within a year or two," says Richard Lawrence, president of Marketing Intelligence Service (MIS), a new product tracking firm in Naples, New York. Household products are a favorite green target. According to MIS, the category accounted for 16 percent of the green entries last year.[4]

Between now and the year 2000, it is unlikely that any consumer attitude shift will have a more dramatic impact on product

marketing than the public's growing environmental consciousness. Today there are many striking examples of the significant
competitive advantages that can be won by taking a proactive
stance in this highly visible area. For example, the hottest items in
the detergent category right now are new ultra detergents that
concentrate the same cleaning power in boxes half the size of their
predecessors.

Other notable examples are hypoallergenic or chemical-free
line extensions that are popping up across a wide spectrum of
products from detergents to cosmetics. These line extensions
come at the environmental issue from an internal rather than an
external perspective. As such they are designed to address consumers' safety concerns about repeated exposure to irritating or
toxic substances. Throughout the marketing world today, managers who are serious about business growth are earmarking a
large percentage of their product development resources for work
in the environmental area.

Significance for Megabrands

Obviously the three key trends just discussed—demographic,
life-style, and attitude shifts—can create line extension opportunities for all brands, regardless of size. However, these trends
hold out the largest opportunities for megabrand marketers. Because they are operating off a bigger base, megabrand marketers
can introduce a greater number of line extensions without under-
mining the base business. Smaller competitors must be more cau-
tious in the number and frequency of line extensions or run the
risk of fragmenting their business into many vulnerable pieces.

STEP 3: DEVELOPING THE PRODUCTS

Having identified general opportunity areas, marketers must next
turn their attention to the development of the actual line extensions that will take best advantage of these opportunities. To be
successful, these line extensions must customize or repackage the
base brand's benefit and make it more appealing to specific user
groups. As a result, consumers within these groups must perceive the line extension's performance to be significantly enhanced versus the base product and more appropriate for their
particular needs.

In the past most line extensions tended to offer enhanced performance on a primary benefit dimension. However, in today's developed markets, perceived performance superiority is most often achieved by attaching, or bundling, a secondary benefit to the primary benefit provided by the base brand. In such cases the resulting performance improvements are not significant enough to be measured objectively in a research laboratory. Yet because of the subjective importance of these secondary benefits to specific target groups, these benefit bundles are often perceived as being superior overall.

When considering product development opportunities, it is useful to remember that most consumer product line extensions fall into three general classes. These three classifications can provide a template for line extension development. By focusing idea-generation activities within these categories, the efficiency and productivity of the product development process can be greatly enhanced. The three classes of line extensions include:

1. Formula variations.
2. Aesthetic variations.
3. Variations in product form.

Not included here are simple variations in package size or composition (e.g., bottles versus cans). Likewise, different flavor and recipe variations of food and beverage products are normally considered components of the base brand business and not distinct line extensions in their own right.

Formula Variations

The most obvious and often the most significant line extension opportunities are those that offer straightforward variations of the base brand's formula. These formula variations usually involve:

1. A stronger, more intense version of the base brand's primary benefit.

2. A reduced, gentler version of the primary benefit.

3. A combination of the primary benefit plus a primary benefit from a related category.

Stronger (extra-strength) line extensions are common across many product categories. These products take many forms, from extra-strength pain relievers to moisturizers for extra-dry skin to chunky soups for men with big appetites. While the product descriptors may vary, these line extensions all offer consumers a more intense experience of the base brand's primary benefit. In other words, *more* of a good thing.

At the other end of the spectrum are line extensions that reduce or lessen some aspect of the base brand's benefit in a way that makes the product more appealing to many consumers. For example, diet sodas or light beers provide a taste experience similar to the base product, without as many calories. In the shampoo category, special formulas for extra-fine hair offer gentler cleaning properties. In the cosmetics and toiletries business, it is not uncommon to find entire lines of products built around different potency levels (e.g. suntan lotions, facial cleansing products, etc.).

Finally line extension formula variations often provide the base brand's primary benefit augmented or combined with a primary benefit from a related category. This list of combination line extensions is very long and includes such products as shampoos plus conditioners, detergents with fabric softeners, cleaners with disinfectants, and deodorant soaps. While these combination products were originally designed to appeal to consumers on the basis of added convenience, they are regularly perceived as being more effective.

Aesthetic Variations

The second general class of line extensions can be defined as aesthetic improvements. These products bundle a base brand's primary benefit with a secondary aesthetic benefit—most often a new scent, design, or color. While aesthetic improvements are not intended to serve any utilitarian function, they can contribute importantly to the consumer's perception of the brand's efficacy. Lemon-scented household cleaning products offer a good example. While these line extensions are widely believed to clean more effectively, their cleaning power is exactly the same as regular-scent products.

Designer paper towels and facial tissues are two more examples of aesthetic line extensions. In these instances, the visual appeal of the decorative designs motivate substantial numbers of consumers to purchase these items over the less expensive but less interesting plain white variety.

Variations in Product Form

Today the third class of line extension—product form—probably offers the greatest opportunities for new-product development. As previously mentioned, it is important to make a clear distinction between simple packaging and product form. The primary purpose of packaging is to house and preserve a product from the time of manufacturing to the time of purchase. An important secondary purpose is to attract attention at retail. The primary purpose of product form is to enhance the use of a product itself.

By product form we mean the shape or configuration in which a product is delivered to consumers. A glimpse into just about any category will reveal a wide variety of product forms. For example, in the nonprescription drug business, it is normal to find major brands available in tablet, capsule, and liquid form. In the antiperspirant category most major brands are sold in stick, roll-on, and spray configurations. A representative detergent line would include a powder, a liquid, and a concentrated powder.

New product forms can become powerful line extensions. In some cases product forms can actually improve product performance. For instance, a roll-on antiperspirant is truly more effective than a spray because it permits high levels of ingredients to be applied directly to the skin. As such the roll-on delivery system itself improves product performance. Similarly a liquid detergent can be more effective at removing tough stains than a powder because it can be poured directly onto the stain.

In other cases product form can create the perception of superior performance, even where it does not exist. In nonprescription drugs, consumers perceive capsules to be more effective than tablets of equivalent strength. While capsules have grown to become the most popular form of extra-strength medications, in reality, tablets provide speedier relief because they dissolve more quickly in the digestive system.

Innovations in product form can also provide real consumer advantages in convenience. Instant coffee provides coffee drinkers with a quick, no-mess method for satisfying a caffeine craving. Prepared puddings in sealed, individualized servings allow parents to serve their children tasty desserts with no preparation. Occasionally the added convenience of product form innovations are so dramatic that they create whole new categories and brands (e.g., spray cleaners and microwave popcorn). In product development as in life itself, the line between form and substance is often blurred. For this reason, form innovations have played a major role in the development of every consumer category.

STEP 4: EVALUATING THE UPSIDE

After generating a series of new-product concepts by applying the matrix approach described above, marketers must skillfully evaluate these opportunities. New product testing is a complex undertaking. As such every company utilizes its own unique evaluation system. Although it is not possible to discuss the intricacies of each system in this chapter, it is appropriate to review the three primary steps that are included in virtually every approach. These three steps are:

1. Qualitative screening.
2. Concept/product testing.
3. Purchase laboratories, test marketing, or both.

Generally preliminary qualitative testing involves focus groups and one-on-one interviews in which consumers are exposed to rough concept statements and then probed for their reactions. Based on the input from these sessions, the marketing team must make subjective judgments about the relative appeal of the various concepts. Once a decision is made, only the strongest of the concepts is taken to the next stage of testing. Of the remainder, some are reworked while others are abandoned.

Within most major companies, the second step in the evaluation process is quantitative concept/product testing. In this research a projectable sample of target consumers representative of the country at large is exposed to the new line-extension concept, and interest is measured on a variety of key dimensions. Next, consumers are given prototype samples of the new product and asked to use these for a specified period of time. At the end of this test, their reactions are measured again. Over the years marketers have established reliable benchmark scores for each step in this process. When a new line extension meets or exceeds the benchmarks, it moves ahead. When it does not, it is back to the drawing board for further refinement.

The final step in the evaluation process is testing the new product within the competitive context. Historically this has often meant placing the new item in a representative set of real-world test markets and tracking its performance over an extended period of time—usually one year or longer. Today, for many reasons including lack of confidentiality, fewer companies are utilizing this traditional approach.

In place of test markets, many organizations are now relying on simulated test markets or purchase laboratories. These procedures make use of simulated shopping situations and sophisticated computer modeling to project sales volume and market share. Although the precision of these projections is often highly debatable, most companies believe that market simulations can provide a ballpark estimate of a new item's volume potential.

As a final, fail-safe step, companies that use market simulations will often introduce a proven new item into select lead markets in advance of the national rollout. This step can help uncover any hidden problems with the sales force or the retail trade and correct them prior to the national introduction. However, to be effective, lead markets must be evaluated quickly. If these introductions extend beyond a few months, competitive advantage can be lost.

STEP 5: FILLING THE PIPELINE

The product development matrix described in this chapter is powered by demographic, life-style, and consumer attitudinal currents. Therefore, keeping these currents flowing is critical to the success of any long-term product development effort. In practical terms this means identifying significant changes in these three important areas and responding to them in advance of the competition.

To be successful, major marketers cannot depend exclusively on trend watchers such as the *Yankelovich Monitor*, that can be studied by any interested party. They must also take steps to supplement these public sources with proprietary information of their own. In recent years this need for additional, proprietary insight has created a new category of marketing consultants—the futurists—who bring with them a full array of trend-tracking tools.

Life-Style Focus Groups

One of the favorites in the futurists' tool kit is the traditional consumer focus group—but with a broad life-style rather than a product spin. In a recent interview, trend spotter Judith Langer commented on the unique value of trend-watching groups. She stated, "In some ways qualitative research is better than survey research as a trend-spotting tool. With survey research, a researcher must suspect that a new trend is occurring in order to frame a question. In qualitative research, the researcher doesn't have to ask the right questions. Respondents can volunteer what's on their minds."[5]

In surveying the marketplace for new trends, researchers like Langer have discovered that certain cities regularly serve as important bellwethers. As a result these cities are regular sites for life-style focus groups. According to Langer, "Typically, qualitative studies are conducted in markets where new trends start, such as New York City and Los Angeles. They are also held in more 'middle America' markets that are slower to adopt a change. But these markets also have their trend-leaders and followers. The vanguard tells you what's new; the mainstream separates the real trends from the fads."[6]

Media Analysis

Another effective and as-yet not widely used method of identifying emerging trends is media content analysis. Originally developed in the 1930s, content analysis is based on the premise that the media will report emerging trends in advance of broad public consciousness of these trends. As coverage grows, so too will consciousness. However, there will be a "lead-lag" relationship between the two.

John Merriam, a consultant and co-author of *Trend Watching: How the Media Creates Trends and How to Be the First to Uncover*

Them, has provided some additional thoughts about how media content analysis can be effectively utilized. Merriam states,

> In some cases, it is possible to develop "trend streams" by thinking about publications in terms of their readers. Thus, ideas about diet and nutrition are published first in technical journals. The coverage then moves through popular-science magazines and wellness newsletters to diet magazines, and daily newspapers, and finally mass market magazines like *Redbook* and *Reader's Digest*.
>
> The public's knowledge of the value of fiber in the human diet is a good example of how a trend stream works. Reports on the benefits of fiber first appeared in scientific journals. By the time these reports reached magazines sold at supermarkets, cereal manufacturers were well on top of the trend.[7]

Whether the chosen approach is focus groups, media analysis, or some more esoteric form of computer forecasting, major brand managers must be constantly exploring innovative ways to monitor consumer trends in order to keep ideas flowing through the product development pipeline and take the offensive in the line extension game.

Ongoing, aggressive line extension is the means by which a major brand is transformed into a megabrand. In today's competitive markets, there is no standing still. When it comes to developing the product line, the choice is stark and simple: Innovate and move ahead; or copy and fall behind.

NOTES

1. Peter F. Drucker, *Innovation and Entrepreneurship: Practice and Principles* (New York: Harper & Row, 1985), pp. 95–96.
2. "Home Alone with $660 Billion," *Business Week*, July 29, 1991, p. 76.
3. Rebecca Piirto, "Measuring Minds," *American Demographics*, December 1990, p. 32.
4. "The Long Winding Road to a Cleaner, Safer Planet," *Super-Brands 1990*, supplement to *Adweek*, p. 54.
5. Judith Langer, "Secrets of the Trend Spotters: Focus Groups." *American Demographics*, February 1991, p. 38.
6. Ibid., p. 39.
7. Ibid., p. 40.

Chapter Six

Leveraging the Spending

Over 2,000 years ago, the Greek mathematician Archimedes is reputed to have said, "Give me a lever and a place to stand, and I will move the world."

With this statement Archimedes became the first human being to formally articulate the principle of leverage. Today this same principle, originally used to describe a phenomenon in the physical world, is used routinely to describe a similar phenomenon in the abstract world of business and marketing. However, its meaning is still the same:

Leverage is gaining the maximum effect with the minimum effort.

In the marketing world today, a major product line is ideally positioned to exert tremendous leverage against its designated target groups. This leverage can be generated by utilizing the fulcrum of an established customer base and the lever of a focused, total line marketing program. However, to paraphrase Archimedes, before this leverage can be successfully applied, the business must know where to stand.

In recent years, as the emphasis has shifted from new products to line extensions, the potential spending leverage of a major product line has dramatically increased. This increase is not only a function of pure size. It is also a result of the special, symbiotic relationship that exists between a base brand and its line extensions. However, in order to take full advantage of this relationship, marketers must abandon many of the traditional ways of thinking about line extensions and marketing support.

HOLISTIC APPROACH

To realize maximum leverage, managers of major product lines must undergo a change in mind-set and begin to take a holistic approach to marketing. In other words they can no longer think of a product line in a linear fashion, with each item perceived as a separate point. Rather, they must begin to view individual items as *both separate and connected* at the same time, *both distinct parts and representatives of the entire line*. In this regard they can be guided by the thinking of leading-edge innovators in biology, computer science, and other technology-driven fields who are literally revolutionizing those disciplines.

In his book *Future Perfect*, MIT professor Stanley Davis discusses the holistic outlook and its origins in the biological sciences. In describing the holistic model, Davis states,

> "In the mechanistic model the irreducible element is the part, in the holistic model it is the whole. The whole is not merely the sum of the parts, nor can it be comprehended in an additive way, gradually. It has to be apprehended in the same way that it is composed, instantly.
>
> Not only is the whole considered greater than, and different from, the sum of its parts, but the whole can also be interspersed in all of its parts. Arthur Koestler coined the word "halon" for something that has the characteristics of being both a part and a whole at the same time. As such, it has both an integrative tendency and an autonomous aspect. Consider our genetic code. The code for our entire biology is in every one of our cells.[1]

According to Davis, the holistic model and the kind of breakthrough thinking it inspires is beginning to find practical applications in many innovative business organizations. For those marketers who grasp the implications of this new paradigm for their business, the opportunities that it presents for leveraging spending are enormous. For example, if every item in a major product line is a "halon" and therefore represents both a distinct part and the larger whole, marketers can, to a large degree, support the whole line by supporting a particular item.

No longer must they adhere to predictable tactics and rigid formulas that allocate marketing support in direct proportion to sales volume. With the flexibility provided by a holistic outlook, marketers can now feel confident shifting substantial support away from large, declining line items to new items with high growth potential. By taking a holistic approach, they can now perceive more clearly how a new item *and* the entire line benefit from such a shift.

Like any breakthrough idea, this approach must be tempered by real-world realities. Nonetheless, it is a paradigm shift whose time has come. Today, managers of many of America's most successful product lines are intuitively and consciously grasping this new reality. As they do so, they are applying the massive financial resources of major brands to leverage growth opportunities within the line, while supporting mature items with reduced, cost-efficient programs.

COMMON POSITIONING

What makes a holistic approach viable for major-brand marketing is the fact that every product in the line shares a common heritage. Each is built off the same basic positioning and each offers variations of the same rational and emotional core benefits. This common positioning creates opportunities for synergy across every component of a major brand's marketing program. For reasons that will be discussed later, the potential synergies are greatest in the area of consumer advertising. They are most difficult to achieve at retail, where companies must offer lucrative allowances on all items to maintain distribution and trade support.

During the 90s it is apparent that a major philosophical shift is underway within the marketing community. Product managers are recognizing the benefits of the holistic outlook and are actively seeking synergies across their lines. Increasingly they are taking a "forest" rather than a "tree" approach to major-brand marketing. They are also recognizing that it is in the long-term interest of the line to nurture the strong, young saplings rather than to continue lavishing nutrients on established adults.

In today's tough, competitive environment, the need for spending efficiency is universal. However, the importance of spending leverage is particularly critical for managers striving to build major brands into megabrands. To triumph over sizable competitors, there can be little wasted motion. Instead, marketers must consistently attain the biggest bang for their bucks. The section that follows provides a step-by-step approach for leveraging the marketing spending of a major product line. In particular the discussion will cover three major topics:

1. Supporting the existing line.
2. Introducing new items.
3. Avoiding the pitfalls.

By following the spending recommendations under each of these headings, managers can take a giant step towards making their marketing programs more productive and earning a greater return on their advertising and promotion investments.

SUPPORTING THE EXISTING LINE

Changing marketplace conditions have dramatically increased the cost of doing business in America's largest consumer categories today. While size alone endows major product lines with bigger marketing war chests than smaller competitors, a high level of absolute spending by itself doesn't guarantee success. There must also be efficiency in the allocation of spending support on a line item basis. In developing an efficient spending program for an existing product line, the first step is to distinguish those line items that represent the basic underpinnings and key building blocks of the franchise from the entries that do not provide fundamental, structural support.

The keystone of a major product line is the base or parent brand. As the name implies, the base brand is the progenitor of all the products in the line. It is the source of the line's identity and strength. To ensure the long-term health of a major franchise, it is imperative that the base brand be supported by competitive levels of spending. However, as the line continues to grow and evolve, the type of spending support placed behind the base brand may shift from an emphasis on advertising to a heavier reliance on sales promotion.

The basic building blocks of the product line will be referred to as *major line extensions*. To optimize growth, major line extensions require separate, ongoing spending support. The other entries in the line will be referred to as *minor line extensions*. Once established, most minor line extensions can be effectively supported by the base brand's marketing expenditures. In distinguishing between the majors and the minors, it is important to recognize that while size is an important criterion, it is not the critical, distinguishing characteristic of a major line item.

Major versus Minor Line Extensions

A major line extension offers a significant variation of the base brand's core benefit.

As a result of this benefit variation, a major line extension is able to significantly broaden the appeal of the product line. Because it is perceived by the consumer as being significantly different on an important dimension, it has the ability to attract large numbers of new users into the brand franchise. In view of the potential of these products to significantly expand the business, major line extensions merit substantial, item-specific marketing support for a prolonged period of time.

For example, Diet Coke is a major line extension within the Coca-Cola line. It provides a significant variation of Classic Coke's core benefit (i.e., similar taste/reduced calories). From the time of its introduction, Diet Coke has been supported by separate, item-specific advertising and promotion programs. Because of its important benefit variation and separate marketing support, Diet Coke has succeeded in attracting many new users into the Coke franchise.

By contrast,

A minor line extension offers only minor variations of the base brand's core benefit.

Since consumers perceive these items as providing essentially the same benefits as the base brand, they do not have the same potential to attract large numbers of new users into the brand franchise. Because their message is similar to the base product and their incremental volume potential is small, they usually do not require additional support apart from the base brand's program.

Ban floral-scent antiperspirant is an example of a minor line extension. Apart from aesthetics it provides no significant benefit versus regular Ban. As a result, except for a brief burst of introductory advertising, it has received no separate support. Such limited support of minor line extensions is common practice in consumer products marketing. Since the product variations themselves are limited, such products can quickly be folded into the base brand's marketing effort.

Zero-Based Budgeting

In the past, managers of major product lines have attempted to develop rigid formulas for setting marketing budgets based on sales and market share. One area where this formulaic approach was particularly evident was consumer advertising. For years, many marketers followed the old adage that "a brand's share of advertising spending should equal its share of market." As such, if a brand had a 20 percent category share and the total category ad spending was $100 million, then that brand was expected to allocate $20 million for consumer advertising.

Always on shaky ground, such theoretical formulas have been largely abandoned by contemporary marketers. Now marketing budgets are put together based on real-world experience and a careful analysis of past performance. Once set, these budgets are adjusted regularly to reflect actual sales results and marketplace conditions. In establishing marketing budgets for a major product line, most managers today favor a zero-based approach based on history and practical experience.

As the name suggests, the zero-based approach calls for a critical examination of every element in the spending plan. There are no exceptions. On an item-by-item basis, managers review what has worked in the past and what changes are anticipated in the future in the area of competitive activity or other extraneous conditions that might be expected to impact the business. Then they build the budgets from the ground up for each product in the line.

Base-Brand Spending

For many extended product lines, the zero-based budgeting procedure results in the base brand receiving a low level of support as a percentage of total sales. This phenomenon occurs for two reasons. First, because of its substantial market share, the base brand has achieved a critical volume mass that creates spending efficiencies versus smaller products. Secondly, the base brand is by definition a mature business and therefore in a maintenance marketing mode. Experience has shown that it is much less costly to maintain current users than to go out and attract completely new ones.

The principal exception to this rule is the case of a major product improvement in the base brand. Such an improvement provides the base product with the means of attracting new users from competitive brands. In most instances this opportunity is short-lived, since competitors are likely to match the product upgrade as quickly as possible. Nonetheless, savvy marketers recognize the importance of maximizing any base-brand performance advantage, no matter how fleeting, with incremental marketing support.

In most cases a higher percentage of base-brand spending is devoted to promotion rather than advertising. This occurs because the majority of consumers are already aware of the base brand's benefits through years of advertising support. Once established, considerably less spending is required to maintain consumer awareness than to build it from scratch. However, in today's highly competitive commodity categories, even mature base brands must continue to make heavy investments in promotional spending to maintain their positions.

To hold on to their customers, base brands must offer ongoing promotional incentives to encourage repeat purchase. Otherwise, consumers may be lured out of the franchise by a competitor's offer. In addition, the retail trade demands lucrative allowances to keep products on their shelves and to back them with the special price features that are essential to major brand success. In most product line marketing budgets, trade promotion is the single largest line item. This is particularly true for established base brands.

Existing Line Extensions

In the zero-based budgeting process, managers of successful product lines usually earmark separate, ongoing marketing support for major line extensions. As previously discussed, a major line extension represents a business within a business, with its own specialized benefits and distinct user base. In today's super-segmented markets, major line extensions also compete for customer loyalty with similar products in competitive lines. For all of these reasons, they require independent marketing spending in order to prosper.

On a ratio basis (spending/sales), a major line extension usually requires more aggressive spending support than the base brand. This additional support is merited for two reasons: First, from a chronological perspective, a line extension is a next-generation product, competing in a newer segment of the market. If sales in this segment are still rising, then the line extension has a better opportunity to attract new users than the base brand, which may be competing in a flat or declining market segment. Therefore, more aggressive marketing support is often justified to take advantage of this new business opportunity.

Second, the relative size of a major line extension puts it at a spending disadvantage versus the base product. Although the sales volume of most major line extensions is smaller than the base business, the level of marketing spending required to support these sales does not fall off proportionately. In every category competitive pressures create threshold levels of advertising and promotion spending. Regardless of absolute size, a product's support spending cannot be allowed to fall below these thresholds if the product is to succeed. As a result support ratios for major line extensions are usually higher than for base brands.

As discussed earlier, it is not cost efficient to provide minor line extensions with separate marketing support beyond the introductory period. In some cases marketers choose to maintain awareness of these products by featuring them in a brief "tag" at the end of commercials for other products in the line. More often these products are supported only indirectly by line advertising and promotional activities.

Computer Modeling

In recent years marketers have been able to fine-tune zero-based budgeting calculations through the application of sophisticated computer modeling techniques. These techniques allow brand managers to experiment with an infinite range of what-if spending scenarios. They can simulate the impact of virtually any conceivable change in the marketing mix, including major increases and decreases in overall spending and the reallocation of spending among various line items. They can even project the impact of changes in a brand's promotional program, or alterations in the levels of advertising support.

By taking a zero-based approach built upon brand history and refined through computer modeling, it is no longer very difficult to establish sound marketing budgets for existing items in a major product line. However, setting the budgets for new line extension introductions is less of a science and more of an art. Yet even with new items, it is possible to formulate effective budgets based on general knowledge and experience with similar products.

INTRODUCING NEW ITEMS

In the past some marketers chose to take a sink-or-swim approach to new line extension introductions. In essence their preferred tactic was to throw it in the marketplace and see if it floats. Despite the lack of substantial marketing support, some products did miraculously manage to stay on the surface. But even in less demanding days gone by, the vast majority of unsupported new items sank like stones—never to be seen again. In today's complex and competitive markets, new line extension introductions require special marketing support if they are to have any chance for success.

In view of the millions of dollars required to establish a new line extension today, it is unrealistic to expect that the product's first year sales will generate adequate funds to cover marketing expenses. While spending shortfalls are particularly evident with minor line extensions, even major line extension sales are sometimes inadequate to underwrite large-scale marketing programs. To solve this problem, managers must abandon a pay-as-you-go approach to a new item launch. To maximize the volume potential of new line extensions, incremental funding must be supplied from other sources.

The Miracle of Leverage

When it comes to underwriting marketing costs for a new line extension, a major product line can often offer miraculous leverage. By judiciously shifting monies from established line items to the new product, marketing expenditures associated with the introduction can be effectively subsidized, while spending for the overall line can be held constant. At the same time, for reasons that will be discussed shortly, the spending shift can be accomplished without diminishing the effectiveness of the established brand's marketing programs. In fact, contrary to conventional wisdom, the impact of the total line effort can actually be dramatically heightened!

Unlike new brand-name introductions, which require heavy investment spending with resultant declines in corporate profits, line-extension launches require minimal investment spending with only minimal impact on the bottom line. From the standpoint of the corporation, this procedure is particularly appealing because it allows a company to have its cake and eat it too. By reallocating marketing monies within the line, managers can effectively leverage the new-product opportunity without ratcheting up the costs.

It almost sounds too good to be true, but this approach is neither a trick performed with lights and mirrors nor a Ponzi pyramid destined to come crashing down under its own weight. It is a legitimate, proven spending strategy that has been used time and time again to build major product lines. It works because of the special, holistic qualities of a major product line. These qualities present exceptional opportunities in the area of marketing communications.

Advertising

Of all the elements in the marketing plan, advertising presents the greatest opportunity for spending leverage. Within major product lines, base brands enjoy high levels of consumer awareness. This awareness is the cumulative result of many successive years of advertising and promotional expenditures. Apart from announcing periodic product news, such as product improvements, the purpose of base-brand advertising is to *maintain* this awareness.

Once built, brand awareness erodes very slowly. In many respects this erosion process is analogous to stopping a huge supertanker. It takes a long time! The extended half-life of advertising awareness is one of the principal reasons marketers can temporarily divert advertising funds from an established brand to a new line extension—without adversely affecting the existing product over the short term. In the past there have been numerous examples of established products that have funded new-product advertising from their own advertising budgets without suffering any measurable negative effects.

On the surface it would appear that such an on again–off again pattern of advertising support would have a corrosive effect on established brand awareness over time. Yet, although most major product lines have applied this spending strategy on numerous occasions, consumer awareness of these products has never been higher. Therefore, something more fundamental must be at work that is preventing this decline.

That something is the holistic aspect of product line advertising. Because of the holistic qualities of a major product line, reallocating support from an established brand to a new line extension is not the same as curtailing support. In fact it is qualitatively different. Reallocating support does not reduce the level of brand name advertising by one iota. It simply shifts the focus from one product in the line to another. The brand name is maintained in the public consciousness as strongly as before.

In this situation, users of the base brand are *still* reminded of the base product every time they are exposed to an ad for the new line extension. Needless to say, they are not exposed to the brand's specific sales message. However, assuming they are already familiar with the base product and its benefits, this loss of sales message specificity will have little negative short-term effect.

The Halo Effect

Some experts believe there may actually be an additional, "bonus" benefit to the reallocation strategy. Recent studies strongly suggest that shifting base-brand advertising support to a new item may have a beneficial halo effect on the base product. The halo effect refers to the positive rub-off that advertising for a new item can impart to the older members of the product line.

Currently the dynamics of this halo effect are not completely understood. One hypothesis suggests that consumers may mentally transfer the "news" and contemporary image of the new entry to the other products in the line. But whatever the reasons, research is confirming that consumers tend to rank the older products in a product line more favorably after a new item introduction. As such their *perceptions* of these products' performance improves significantly, even though *actual* performance does not.

Not surprisingly, the halo effect is strongest in the case of a minor line extension. Since the primary benefit of such a product is very similar to the base brand, advertising for a minor line extension can effectively recall and reinforce advertising for the base product. In many respects the campaigns are interchangeable. For example, an advertisement for Crest pump toothpaste also sells the benefits of regular Crest toothpaste. Similarly, an ad for Extra-Strength Tylenol Gelcaps also promotes the benefits of Extra-Strength Tylenol tablets.

Consumer Promotion

Just as the reallocation of advertising funds can be a potent short-term marketing strategy to support new entries within a line, so too can this same strategy be utilized in another area of marketing communication—consumer promotion. However, in this instance, the leverage provided by the existing product is more limited because money, not brand image, is the primary currency.

For established components of a major product line, the primary purpose of consumer promotion is to maintain users by encouraging regular, repeat purchase. This objective is usually achieved by providing consumers with regular cash incentives to purchase the product throughout the year. Yet there is a built-in inefficiency in these efforts. Because many regular consumers would purchase these products anyway without added incentives, the "wastage" factor for many promotions, particularly cents-off coupons, is very high.

Conversely the primary goal of consumer promotion for a new line item is to encourage initial trial. Since the new product is starting from ground zero, there is virtually no wastage in the early stages. Any trial is a new trial in the opening months of a product launch. What's more, because of the interest generated by the new offering, trial incentives for a new product have a higher probability of attracting nonbrand users into a franchise than comparable incentives for existing products.

By reducing the level of promotion activity for established line items and shifting funding to new entries, the promotion program of a major product line can be leveraged effectively. However, this exercise should be undertaken with considerable caution—one small step at a time. For if a product line succeeds in attracting new users through promotion of a new item but loses greater numbers of current users as a result of promotional cutbacks for the base brand, it ends up losing significant ground. As such this leaky-bucket approach to product-line marketing is destined to come up dry.

Trade Promotion

In the area of trade promotion and dealing, there is usually much less line leverage. This is the case because the trade demands a particular level of promotional allowances to maintain brand distribution and provide the regular features and displays that are critical to established brand sales. In addition, the trade frowns on any move that "robs Peter to pay Paul" by shifting support from established products to new items.

Unfortunately for marketers, total trade promotion spending almost always increases when new items are introduced. In addition to heavy introductory allowances, special promotions such as slotting allowances and failure fees are often required to obtain distribution. Far from offering opportunities for spending efficiencies, trade promotion is the most inefficient component of a line's marketing spending. As such, every effort should be made to manage these costs as closely as possible.

Timing

When attempting to leverage the combined spending power of a major product line, timing is everything. While the reallocation of support funds can be extremely effective during a rapid growth phase, the point of diminishing returns is eventually reached. In the case of consumer advertising, this point comes when incremental spending no longer results in incremental consumer awareness. In consumer promotion the point occurs when additional programs do little to increase product trial.

Once the new business potential of a line extension has been realized, incremental marketing spending for this item should cease and support should again be allocated in proportion to sales. Failure to return to a spending/sales equilibrium will place the established business at serious risk.

Ultimately both the amount and duration of incremental marketing support are directly linked to protected sales volume. A major line extension can warrant a prolonged reallocation of the base brand's marketing funds since the new product has the potential to attract new franchise users and increase overall line sales. Conversely, because the potential of most minor line extensions to attract new users is small, the majority of these products do not merit incremental line spending beyond the initial six months.

However, it is important to note one key exception—those minor line extensions whose benefit variations are perceived by consumers to improve product performance. These products can offer significant competitive advantages and should receive more extended line support. Ironically the tendency among many manufacturers is to withdraw incremental support prematurely, before maximum line extension growth has been achieved. To optimize growth, companies must resist the temptation to "protect" the base business by shifting spending back to these products too soon.

The following table provides some basic guidelines to assist in the reallocation of marketing funds from the base business in support of a new line extension launch:

Marketing Support for New Line Extensions

	Average Period of Incremental Support (months)
Major	18–24
Minor	12–18
(improved perception of efficacy)	
Minor (other)	1–6

A Balancing Act

In the final analysis the amount of money a manager of a major product line has to work with is a function of the line's sales and profit. Yet for most major product lines today, the availability of marketing dollars is not the basic issue. Rather, the fundamental question is one of spending efficiency or return on marketing investment. To be successful, managers must constantly ask themselves: Will funds invested against established products or reallocated to new-product introductions generate greater returns in the form of incremental sales and profits?

In the constant flux of the marketing world, a product line is always in motion. At any given time, some items in the line are growing, others are enjoying a healthy maturity, and the remainder have entered a period of decline. As a result, product managers are constantly engaged in a balancing act, attempting to place maximum spending support against high-growth opportunities while adequately maintaining the rest of the business. Over time, some will be extremely successful while others will exercise poor judgment, lose their balance, and fall.

AVOIDING THE PITFALLS

In attempting to leverage the spending of a major product line, there are two dangerous pitfalls that managers must carefully avoid. Ironically, both problems are by-products of too much success. The first is overleveraging the line and, thereby, attempting to do too much with too little. The second is becoming complacent and believing that a brand is immune to competitive threats by virtue of its size and dominant market position.

The most common expression of overleveraging is the umbrella advertising campaign. As the name suggests, an umbrella campaign seeks to cover an entire product line with a single advertising effort. In their attempt to say something about everything, umbrella campaigns often end up saying nothing about anything. Consequently such campaigns seldom work. Umbrella campaigns grow out of a distorted understanding of spending leverage. Rather than focusing line spending on important product differences to stimulate sales, they usually depress sales by squandering money behind a bland, generalized message.

While marketers who expect too much leverage out of line spending are often greedy, those who grow complacent about competitive threats are often lazy. As a product line's position becomes more dominant, some managers become accustomed to low spending ratios and high profit margins. As this occurs, there is also a growing inclination to believe that a dominant brand is impervious to most competitive threats. In combination these two attitudes can be disastrous!

How many times have market leaders let competitors get their foot in the door by not responding aggressively to a competitive new-product launch? Once in, it is always a more difficult job to dislodge them. Savvy marketers who respond aggressively to competitive entries often find they reap a double reward. Not only do they thwart a would-be competitor, they also pump up their market share as a result of their defensive programs. With the competitor eliminated, they are often able to maintain these newly found users for many years.

The spending leverage of a large product line is a marvelous marketing tool. If managers are wise and know how to use and not abuse it, this leverage can play a pivotal role in stimulating outstanding line growth and converting major brands into mega-brands.

NOTE

1. Stanley M. Davis, *Future Perfect* (Reading, Mass.: Addison-Wesley, 1987), p. 201.

Chapter Seven

Executing the Marketing Plan

The final step in the process of successfully marketing a major product line is executing the marketing plan itself. It is here that all the strategizing, planning, and development must come together in an integrated, coherent program. When properly executed over a period of years, well-conceived plans become the means by which a major brand is ultimately transformed into a megabrand.

When asked what makes a particular work of art a masterpiece, a famous artist is said to have remarked, "God is in the details." The same response might be appropriate if the question were to be rephrased, What makes a major brand a megabrand? In the end it is the details of the marketing plan that, inch by inch, month by month, and year by year, build share and ultimate market dominance.

The marketing plan for a major product line must be based on the realization that mass marketing, in the traditional sense of the word, is an artifact of the past. Today there are no longer mass markets. Instead there are masses of markets. Just as every item in a line has been customized to satisfy the needs of a particular market segment, so too must every component of a marketing program be customized to effectively reach and motivate distinct consumer groups.

MICROMARKETING WITHIN THE LINE

In reality a major-brand marketing plan should not be one plan at all but, instead, a series of closely integrated plans, each designed to reach specific targets. While many contemporary managers pay lip service to the concept of targeted marketing, they often market every entry in the same broad-scale fashion. Not only is this practice inefficient, it is also highly ineffective.

During the past 10 years, the term *micromarketing* was coined to describe the targeted selling techniques used by marketers of specialized products to reach small customer groups. While the term itself was new, the process itself is actually an extension of accepted marketing practices. In this instance the "spin" is provided by two new developments:

1. A higher reliance on alternative media, such as cable TV, that can reach specialized groups more selectively than the mass media.
2. The application, wherever possible, of new database marketing techniques that can customize communications to individual customers.

Micromarketing techniques were originally developed by the financial services industry and others to reach extremely narrow target segments. In the early years the micromarketer's medium was almost exclusively direct mail. But as the mass media fragmented and became more selective, micromarketers began to move into print, spot TV, and cable. Over the years micromarketers became increasingly sophisticated at reaching very narrow target segments (e.g., households with incomes over $100,000) with finely tuned messages.

Today, to prevail over other large competitors, managers of major product lines must adhere to many of the principles of effective micromarketing. They must apply many of the same attitudes and techniques that have worked so well for smaller marketers to the principal components of their business. Even though the ultimate focus for major-brand marketers is often macro, increasingly, their marketing approach must be micro. To a large extent, they must micromarket within their own lines.

Customized Media

For major-brand marketers, micromarketing has two primary strategic applications. First, it can help make media programs for the individual line items more efficient at reaching their respective target segments. Second, within each target segment it can help make the marketing communications program for line items more effective by customizing messages and promotions for specific consumer groups.

While target segments for major entries within a product line may never be as narrow as traditional micromarketing targets, there are significant demographic differences among these groups. As such, substantial efficiencies can be realized by following a micromarketing approach. For example, age tends to be a discriminating factor among users of various line items, with older elements in the line attracting older users and newer products drawing younger users. There can also be important differences among line item user profiles by geographical region.

To maximize effectiveness, marketers must develop media plans that reach these product user groups as precisely as possible. If necessary, managers must be willing to abandon tried and true media like network television in favor of less familiar media like cable TV. They must be willing to implement innovative regional media programs instead of running the same basic media mix in every part of the nation. Furthermore they must be willing to experiment with alternative media like direct mail that have the ability to reach not only groups of customers but individual customers themselves.

In recent years, particularly in direct mail, there have been some remarkable developments that permit marketers to more finely target the customers of major line items. In a recent article, marketing professor Philip Kotler discussed one of these changes.

The most exciting recent development in consumer marketing is the geo-demographic analysis system (the Prism system by Claritas and the Cluster Plus system by Donnelley are commercial examples) . . . . The developer of the Prism system, Jonathan Robbin, was a computer expert, and also an entrepreneur. Working with census data, he identified 40 socioeconomic groups that make up the lifestyles of the United States. He characterized each by a sobriquet, such as the "fur and station wagon crowd." Robbin's classification is based on the assumption that people in a given area are relatively alike, and that this alikeness shows itself through similar media habits and brand choices. Using his 40 lifestyle groups, you can zero in on zip code areas, or even city blocks, where you'll find the best prospects for your products.[1]

To succeed in today's competitive environment, brand managers must be willing and able to break old, ingrained habits and experiment with unfamiliar media like direct mail. Unfortunately this is often more easily said than done. Inertia is a difficult force to overcome and many conservative corporations are reluctant to move way from tried and true media approaches that have worked well in the past. Nonetheless, as the demassification of the media moves on, so too must its demystification. To be responsive to consumer needs, managers must recognize that the mass media no longer offer the promise, potential, or market penetration of years gone by.

Customized Communications

In addition to media selection, there is a second dimension of micromarketing—the actual marketing communications themselves—that can be extremely effective in marketing major line items. Even within a particular product segment, it is increasingly apparent that a single selling message may not be equally effective with all consumers. This is often due to the growing diversity of our society in both demographics and lifestyle. Marketers who are serious about strengthening the quality of their marketing communications would be well served not to ignore these differences.

According to Professor Kotler,

> Mass marketing in the United States used to aim products at the typical American family, which consisted of a working husband, a homemaker wife, and two children. But today, this "archetypical" American family makes up just 7 percent of the population. . . . In discussions of market segmentation we often hear about manufacturers aiming at women ages 18 to 34, with household incomes over $20,000. In my opinion, the internal heterogeneity of that group makes targeting en masse impossible. Women between 18 and 34 will read quite different magazines, have different lifestyles, different ambitions, and quite different brand preferences.[2]

Some of the most obvious examples of customized communications are the growing number of campaigns aimed at identifiable ethnic groups. Beginning in the 1960s with ground-breaking programs targeted toward blacks, these activities have now expanded to include other ethnic segments. For example, most major marketers today have acknowledged the demographic fact that Hispanics represent at least 10 percent of the U.S. population by developing customized marketing programs for this group. In most cases these programs include customized advertising that utilizes Spanish-language TV and newspapers, as well as special promotions that reflect the values and culture of local Hispanic communities. Often these promotions include special packaging for use in Hispanic neighborhoods.

As Hispanic marketing has gained greater acceptance within the United States, a significant shift in management mind-set has also taken place. Once viewed as an ancillary, expendable activity, managers now perceive Hispanic marketing as an important and integral part of their major-brand marketing programs. As a result they are shifting increasing amounts of dollars away from general marketing budgets to underwrite Hispanic micromarketing efforts.

According to a recent article,

Eyeing that [Hispanic] growth rate, such consumer products heavyweights as Procter & Gamble, McDonald's, and Pepsico and automakers Ford, General Motors, and Toyota are spending millions to reach Hispanic consumers. Although it's still only a tiny fraction of the $130 billion U.S. advertising market, Hispanic ad spending has grown 88 percent over the past five years to $628.2 million, according to *Hispanic Business* magazine.[3]

Experience and success in the Hispanic market has also opened marketers' minds to other ethnic opportunities. Many are now experimenting with specialized programs targeted towards Asians, who now represent a major percentage of the population in many U.S. cities. According to a recent *New York Times* article, "Asian-Americans [are] the fastest-growing minority in the United States, increasing to 6 million last year from 1.5 million in 1970. The number is expected to reach 10 million by the year 2000, quite a bit smaller than the population of Hispanic-Americans, but large enough to attract the attention of many marketers."[4]

For managers of major product lines, the potential for customized communications extends well beyond targeted ethnic programs. Just as consumer markets can be segmented according to demographics and psychographics, so too can brand communications be customized to reflect important distinctions in lifestyles and attitudes. Usually these distinctions are linked to certain critical moments in consumers' lives, such as marriage, a first child, purchase of a home, or retirement. At each of these critical moments, a consumer's informational needs change dramatically. Marketers who customize their communications to reflect these changing needs enjoy a competitive advantage over manufacturers who choose to ignore these differences and deliver the same homogenized message to everyone.

But once again the decision to seriously pursue this type of message customization requires a distinct break with the marketing approaches of the past. To succeed with such a targeted program, marketers must channel substantial money and creative energy away from mainline efforts. Ironically such efforts are often perceived as too dangerous to the base business. In reality the real danger lies in continuing to invest in misdirected communications efforts. The example of new mothers provides a revealing case in point.

For many years marketers have known that the birth of a first child represents a critical moment when purchase patterns for many household products are established. If properly supported, initial purchases by new mothers can be converted into lifelong customer relationships. For example, when new mothers first become heavy consumers of certain products (e.g. bleach), they frequently have many questions about their proper use. These questions can be more effectively addressed through customized communications than through mass advertising.

Yet despite the importance and special needs of this specific group, most marketers direct only token efforts at this critical target segment. By their actions, they deny that this group has any information requirements distinct from the mass audience. In the name of communications efficiencies, they are, in fact, creating avoidable inefficiencies! Across many consumer product catego-

ries today, there remain sizable opportunities for companies willing to break the mold and speak distinctively to new mothers as
well as to other groups at critical life moments through serious,
customized communications programs.

While there is still a long way to go, the seeds of micromarketing have already begun to take hold in the soil of American
business. To varying degrees, managers of large brands have already acknowledged that major items within a product line must
be treated as businesses unto themselves. They are also beginning to appreciate that both the effectiveness and efficiency of
these line-item marketing programs can be further enhanced by
customizing media delivery and message content to reflect important consumer subsegments within these franchises.

But mastering the art of micromarketing is just one step in
successfully executing a major-brand marketing plan. Once all
these "balls" are in the air, managers must keep them moving
through a carefully coordinated marketing program. If managers
lose sight of any of these efforts, they will quickly fall to the
ground. However, if they can keep them moving in a syn-
chronized manner, their ultimate effect can be much more powerful than the sum of the individual parts.

COORDINATING THE PLAN

There is an old saying that "form follows substance." In recent
years the substance of major-brand marketing has undergone
dramatic change. As managers have shifted to a strategy of
growth through line extension, the number of entries in a major-
brand line has multiplied geometrically. As a result of this sub-
stantive change, the form by which companies manage these proliferated products must change as well.

Historically the brand management system was developed to
more aggressively build consumer product franchises. The brand
management system was based on the premise that a brand was
most effectively managed as an independent, freestanding business. The corporation's charge to the brand manager was to develop and execute the most powerful marketing program for each
product. Any issues regarding the impact, either positive or nega-

tive, of these programs on other brands within the corporation was left exclusively for top management to address.

From its inception the lack of a formal structure for coordinating activities among brands was an inherent problem with the classic brand-management system. However, these problems were further exacerbated as focus shifted from marketing many separate brands to marketing megabrands. Today brand managers within major product lines can no longer assume an isolationist attitude nor can they operate with complete autonomy. Since their products share a common brand name, they must also share a common marketing vision.

The successful marketing of these large product lines requires a degree of coordination not necessary in the past. As the substance of consumer products marketing has evolved, the form or structure of the brand management system has also changed. In the leading consumer product companies, this coordination and common vision is provided by a second-generation brand management structure known as the strategic business unit (SBU). The SBU was adopted to acknowledge the marketing interdependence of major line extensions, as well as the overall connectedness of all brands within the same general business area.

THE STRATEGIC BUSINESS UNIT

Although widely used within consumer products companies, the SBU was originally created to manage the activities of a major corporation in the electronics industry. The SBU concept was first developed by McKinsey & Company in its work with GE in the late 1960s. As originally conceived, a business had to meet a number of specific criteria to be designated an SBU. The criteria were as follows:

1. Have a unique business mission, independent of other SBUs.
2. Have a clearly definable set of competitors.
3. Compete in external markets.
4. Be able to carry out integrative planning relatively independently of other SBUs.

5. Be able to manage resources in key areas.
6. Be large enough to justify senior management attention and small enough to serve as a useful focus for resource allocation.

According to strategic planning experts James Gardner, Robert Rachlin, and Allen Sweeney,

> The great strength of the SBU concept lay in its focus on a management style that stressed the strategic position of businesses and the selective allocation of resources for competitive advantage. It sought to do this through deep understanding of each company's businesses and the placement of these businesses in the most relevant "strategic" units for purposes of top-down objective setting, strategy review, and resource allocation.[5]

At most large consumer product organizations today, the SBU sets the framework for major line marketing activity. However, in most cases, the SBU purview is larger than any single category or product line. For example, a company may have an SBU devoted to oral hygiene products whose charter might include not only toothpastes, but mouthwashes, toothbrushes, and dental floss. Actual responsibility for plotting the marketing program of a major toothpaste line would fall to the toothpaste category manager.

The Category Manager

It is the category manager's job to preside over the development of overall objectives and strategies, allocate marketing expenditures across major entries within a line, and set priorities for product development. He or she acts as the linchpin that brings the entire marketing program together. Reporting to the category manager are the senior brand managers for major items within a line. In some cases a category manager may be responsible for more than one major line. But as markets continue to bifurcate between large and small, a company's category presence is increasingly concentrated in one large brand.

While the SBUs in most consumer products companies are marketing-driven, and often marketing-led, the SBU concept extends far beyond the marketing department to include virtually every major unit within the organization. As such, an SBU is a business within a business. In most SBUs a multidisciplined team, including representatives from marketing, sales, market research, finance, manufacturing, and R&D, work together to set objectives and develop programs. This team approach is duplicated at each key management level in the unit from brand manager to SBU manager.

To be effective, these teams must operate in a participative fashion. While each team member brings a specific expertise, all members participate to varying degrees in every aspect of the planning and decision making. Members are encouraged to make contributions across disciplinary lines. Ultimately, when everyone has contributed to the creation of the business plan, everyone is then more committed to making the plan a success.

The integrated thinking fostered by the SBU structure, combined with the personal coordination of the category manager, can effectively meld the diverse micromarketing plans of a major product line into a cohesive whole. But even after priorities have been set, budgets allocated, targets defined, and programs developed, there are still opportunities to make the total line marketing plan more efficient. By utilizing a few simple marketing tactics, the impact of the total brand marketing program can be further enhanced.

If micromarketing provides the approach and the SBU provides the structure, then basic tactics that synchronize the elements of a major-brand marketing plan can heighten the impact of the total program. These are in and of themselves nothing new. In fact they are the same tactics that have been used regularly on an individual brand level for many years. The difference is that they are now being applied to the overall line.

The objective of these tactics is to orchestrate individual marketing events in order to create a heightened line presence with key target audiences—consumers and the trade—on an ongoing basis throughout the year.

ADVERTISING TACTICS

As discussed in an earlier chapter, advertising for an item within a major product line often creates a halo effect that rubs off on other line items. Since all line entries share the same brand name, consumers are often reminded of other line items, particularly the base brand, when exposed to advertising for just one product. The halo effect contains a built-in efficiency for major-brand marketers because it creates the impression of a greater advertising presence and serves to amplify advertising volume. By taking several concrete steps, savvy line marketers can turn this phenomenon even further to their advantage.

Whenever possible, marketers should strive to reinforce the halo effect and thereby strengthen the impact of the overall line advertising program. The objective here is to simultaneously stimulate the line association and tout the benefits of the individual products. Ideally the copy should be working on two levels. The primary communication must, of course, remain the advertised brand's selling message. But on a secondary level, the advertising copy should also evoke associations with the total brand line.

This can be accomplished by weaving common threads into the advertising campaigns for different line items. These unifying devices can range from the very obvious to the very subtle. Some of the more obvious devices include a common signature line, such as "from the makers of," or a musical sign-off. A trademark character, like the Pillsbury Doughboy, who is present in all line commercials is another example of a unifying device. On a more subtle level, advertisers can attempt something less conspicuous like a common spokesperson or a shared visual look across all line campaigns (e.g., a documentary, real-life feeling created through the use of a hand-held camera).

In forging these unifying links, marketers must be careful to maintain the integrity of the individual campaigns. A delicate balance must be struck between reinforcing the common heritage and selling the benefits of each individual product. If restraint is not exercised, it is often easy to lose the all-important brand-selling message in a hazy blur of shared images. However, if done with the correct proportions, a synergy will occur that can heighten the communications impact of each individual effort.

MEDIA TACTICS

Beyond the creative executions, media present a multitude of tactical opportunities for synergies across a major product line. By making use of a few basic scheduling techniques, marketers can increase a line's media profile without raising media budgets by even one penny. Some of these techniques can be utilized to enhance line visibility on a long-term basis over the course of the entire marketing year; others can be employed to provide an immediate boost on a one-time exposure basis. Probably the most significant overall opportunities lie in the area of media flighting.

As previously discussed, rapidly escalating media costs have made it impossible for all but the largest advertisers to maintain a media presence 52 weeks per year. Because of high prices, most advertisers flight their media in on again–off again pulses throughout the year. As costs have risen, the number of weeks most brands are out of advertising has increased substantially.

Clearly this is not a desirable situation for marketers trying to maintain a high profile with their consumers. "Out of sight, out of mind" can be a serious, nagging problem for managers of small brands. But for managers of major product lines, there is a creative solution readily available. The answer is staggering the media schedules of major line items so that some products are out of advertising when others are in. By superimposing one plan on top of another, the gaps in the line's media schedule can be filled and a continuous advertising presence created.

But continuity alone does not an effective media plan make! To break through with consumers, the intensity of the advertising program is also critically important. Once again the flexibility of a major product line affords tremendous advantages over smaller competitors. Commercials or print ads for line items can be packaged or bundled together in a variety of ways to heighten the impact of the overall program.

One high-impact, high-cost approach is program sponsorship. By sponsoring an ongoing program or TV special, marketers have a golden opportunity to advertise a variety of products in close proximity to each other. The collective impact of many commercials from the same product line running together can improve the recall of each individual spot. Likewise in print, an equivalent program such as a special insert in a magazine or newspaper can achieve a comparable effect. The cumulative impact of numerous ads appearing in sequence can significantly improve memorability.

While the rewards of sole sponsorship are considerable, so are the costs. But it is not necessary to be the actual sponsor of a high-impact media vehicle to enjoy similar benefits. For example, a marketer can achieve comparable impact by placing several product line commercials on a single TV program or by scheduling a number of ads back-to-back in the same publication. By employing such tactics, a level of intensity can be achieved that is greater than the ads could generate on their own.

PROMOTION TACTICS

In the promotion area, an extended product line also presents opportunities for tactical synergies. As in media, there is the opportunity to stagger promotions for major line entries so that the trade is promoting the line virtually year-round. This promotional continuity makes it more difficult for competitors, especially smaller brands, to find an opening and to obtain the feature prices, displays, and trade advertising that are so essential to building a business today.

Another trade tactic that has recently emerged is the "flexible" allowance. This permits retailers to pool certain allowances earned on minor line items and apply them to promotions for major, high-volume items. The allowance works to the advantage of large product lines since they can promote their flagship entries even more aggressively. For smaller brands, already at a competitive disadvantage, the flexible allowance can often be the straw that breaks the camel's back, making it too expensive to effectively compete.

Thumb through the insert section of any Sunday newspaper and you'll come across numerous examples of group events—another tactic favored by many marketers. In such cases, various products in the line are drawn together by a common theme or contest. The main beneficiaries of group promotions are the smaller products in a line. Through association with their larger brethren, these products can generate much wider exposure and response than they could expect to achieve operating as independent agents.

Another highly efficient promotional tactic for major product lines is the cross-ruff coupon. In many product categories, the same consumer tends to use a number of different products to perform different functions. This multiple usage presents a perfect opportunity for cross-ruff couponing. By selectively offering users of one line item coupons for other items that complement their current usage pattern, total line business can be increased. What's more, it can be done with great precision and at a very low cost.

PACKAGING

Unlikely though it seems, package design is another area where a large product line can enjoy important tactical advantages. Increasingly, marketers are recognizing that package design plays an important role in the marketing mix. It provides the final stimulus to choose at the actual point of purchase. As such, it is a company's last opportunity to stand apart from the competition and communicate with potential customers. Here, as in the other areas of marketing communications, a major product line can generate important synergies.

In a recent newspaper interview, well-known packaging consultant John Lister discussed the motivations behind managers' growing interest in packaging. According to Lister,

> More and more marketers are realizing that package design is the final stage of their entire marketing effort . . . . What the consumer sees on the supermarket shelf is the last five seconds of your selling effort. It's the stage when the consumer does or does not reach for your product.
>
> There are more than 18,000 different packaged food items in the typical supermarket, 80 percent more than 10 years ago. Yet the average shopping time of 30 minutes has not changed. The upshot: the typical person glances at an average of 10 items a second during a shopping trip, up from 5.5 items a decade ago.[6]

Since a major product line controls a large section of retail shelf space, it should also control a strong position in the last-minute battle for consumer attention. But in order to achieve this position of strength, packaging for the various items within the line must be tied together in a cohesive and reinforcing way. Just as with advertising, there must be a certain family look or shared identity. If line packaging becomes too disjointed and fragmented, the important opportunity for shelf dominance will be lost.

The familiar package of an established base product is a powerful part of a brand's consumer equity that is built through years of product experience. It is what consumers see on the shelf every week when they go shopping. It is what they see every day when they go into their pantries and it is what they pick up every time they use the product. Next to the actual product itself, packaging is as close as consumers can get to a product's true identity. Therefore the base brand's packaging must be the starting point and touchstone for all other packaging within the product line.

Line extensions should attempt to leverage the base brand's packaging equity by retaining many of the critical elements of the base brand's design. Every effort should be made to incorporate the brand's logotype, key design elements, and characteristic colors into line extension packaging. While the line extension packaging must differentiate the product from the rest of the line, it must also retain a clear family look. As a general principle, major line extensions should have a more distinctive look than minor line extensions, since these products provide a more significant variation of the base brand's benefit. This fact should be communicated as clearly in the product's packaging as in its advertising.

When a family look is achieved, the total effect at retail can be stunning. The various components of the product line appear to consumers as both separate and a part of the whole. The overall effect is to convert the retail shelf into one massive billboard for the brand line. This billboard is impossible for consumers to ignore as they move quickly down the supermarket aisles. The billboard can literally overwhelm competitors whose packaging is more fragmented. By creating a family look to line packaging, major product lines can realize yet another tactical advantage over the competition.

RELATIONSHIP MARKETING

A final, yet potentially devastating tactic a major product line can effect against its smaller competitors is relationship marketing. The concept of relationship marketing is an outgrowth of sophisticated computer database technology that allows companies to easily store, access, utilize, and update detailed information about individual consuming households. Simply stated,

Through relationship marketing, a brand strives to create an ongoing personal relationship with an individual customer that extends over many years.

This relationship is created by providing the customer with valuable information or incentives on a regular basis, usually through the vehicle of direct mail. The prototype for all relationship marketing efforts are frequent flier programs. These programs have literally transformed the way business is conducted in the airline industry.

The economics of relationship marketing programs are based on a concept known as *lifetime value*. As the name suggests, lifetime value is the estimated value of an individual customer over the course of his purchasing lifetime. This long-term focus is critical to relationship marketing since the considerable expense of these programs can rarely be justified on a short-term basis. Instead, the payout (and they can pay out handsomely) must be measured over the course of years as loyal consumers come back time and again to purchase a company's brand and assiduously avoid buying competitive products.

As the world of marketing continues to turn in the direction of relationship programs, major product lines will enjoy increasing advantages over smaller brands. The advantages will be based on two principal considerations. First, the absolute cost of these efforts makes it extremely difficult for smaller product lines to ante up the funds required for entry into the game. While they might piggyback with other brands from within their company, the consumer targets are often markedly different. As a result the rationale for combining disparate products into a single program is frequently strained.

Second, and more important, smaller lines seldom offer the range of product choices necessary to sustain a customer relationship over the course of a lifetime. For a relationship marketing program to take hold and succeed, a product line must include an array of products wide enough to satisfy the varied needs of a target household both today and in the future. As the needs of the household continue to evolve, products must continue to be available within the line to satisfy those needs. Otherwise the brand will give up a valuable user and the company will be forced to stand by while a substantial, long-term investment goes down the drain.

For example, consider the major frozen-food line that is perfectly poised to initiate a relationship marketing effort with a young couple. Today the line can offer the couple tasty, low-calorie entrees consistent with their busy, dual-career life-style. When children arrive, they can also provide nutritious family-style frozen meals and easy-to-prepare frozen snacks to keep the kids satisfied between meals. As the couple ages, the line can shift them over to "healthy" low-sodium, low-fat meals for mature adults. What's more, throughout the years it is likely that this relationship household will purchase a number of different products from the same line simultaneously.

As we move toward the year 2000, database-driven relationship marketing is becoming the ultimate tactic for leveraging the marketing plan of many major product lines. When the positioning has been effectively expanded, the line has been fully developed, the spending has been efficiently leveraged, and the marketing program has been properly executed, an aggressive and innovative relationship marketing effort can finally separate a major product line from the rest of the pack. Relationship marketing has the capability to convert a brand from a market leader to a market dominator. As such, it can be the critical tiebreaker that turns a major brand into a megabrand.

NOTES

1. Philip Kotler, "From Mass Marketing to Mass Customization," *Planning Review*, September/October 1989, p. 12.
2. Ibid.

3. Jamie Beckett, "Advertisers Make Pitch to Hispanic Consumers," *San Francisco Chronicle*, April 22, 1991, p. B-1.
4. Michael Lev, "Asian-Americans' Tastes Are Surveyed by Marketer," *The New York Times*, January 14, 1991, p. D-11.
5. James R. Gardner, Robert Rachlin, and H. W. Allen Sweeney, *Handbook of Strategic Planning* (New York: John Wiley & Sons, 1986), p. 19.
6. Anthony Ramirez, "Lessons in the Cracker Market," *The New York Times*, July 5, 1990, p. C-1.

Chapter Eight
Megabrand Case Histories

By the time they reach the national tour, all professional tennis players have mastered the fundamental skills of tennis. Every pro has spent thousands of hours on the court perfecting basic skills and planning strategies. Nonetheless, what separates the top-seeded players from the rest of the pack is their ability to consistently implement those skills and strategies under the constant pressure of day-to-day, real match play.

In identifying the marketing elite from the rest of the field, the same dynamic is at work. Some brands show flashes of great technical brilliance but lack the steadiness and tactical insight to prevail. Likewise, other products seem to have mastered all the basic skills and strategies but cannot seem to muster that special flair or brilliance to prevail in the most challenging competitive situations. Finally there is that select group of megabrands that consistently put it all together. Year after year these brands dominate the competitive field and national rankings.

In the case histories that follow, we will examine the performance of some of these dominant players. As we do this, the insights that have helped these elite brands succeed will become more apparent.

In the preceding chapters, the principles of successful megabrand management were presented and analyzed. In this chapter the discussion will turn from principles to practicalities. A series of actual case histories will illustrate megabrand marketing principles at work in the real world.

The objective is not to provide a comprehensive analysis of each product in all its complexity. Such a task would take volumes to accomplish. Rather, each example will focus on one key principle of successful megabrand marketing.

By themselves each case history illustrates one piece of the total picture. Collectively they represent a broad montage of state-of-the-art marketing in America today.

Because there is often something to be learned from failures as well as from success stories, two case studies of megaflops will also offer insights into what does not work and why.

MEGAHITS

EXPANDING BRAND POSITIONING

Case Study 1: Lysol

For generations Lysol dominated the disinfectant segment of the home cleaning market. The brand's presence was so pervasive that the Lysol brand name and its familiar brown bottle became synonymous with the product class in the minds of American consumers. Early in its development, Lysol's strength also became its limitation. Since the disinfectant segment was small in terms of dollar volume, the brand had to break out of this narrow market niche in order to grow.

By 1990 Lysol had accomplished this objective and then some. Today Lysol has become America's top line of home cleaning products. The brand's dramatic rise can be traced to a series of successful line extension introductions. However, the bedrock of Lysol's success—the strategic insight that made all these line extensions possible—was the skillful expansion of the brand's disinfectant positioning into a much broader competitive context.

As originally defined, Lysol's disinfectant positioning was too restrictive to support a broad line of home cleaning products. Most consumers perceive disinfectants to be specialty items meant to be used sparingly to "kill germs" in restricted areas, such as bathrooms. To provide Lysol with a wider range of potential applications, the parameters of both its rational and emotional benefits had to be enlarged.

Lysol's inspiration was to redefine its rational disinfectant benefit so that it became an essential component of all cleaning activities. By making the case that an object must not only be free of dirt and odors but also free of germs to be truly clean, the brand was able to accomplish its goal. The argument proved both relevant and persuasive to consumers. As a result Lysol found itself with positioning broad enough to support an extended product line.

In recent years Lysol has successfully taken its cleaning/disinfectant benefit into every major segment of the home cleaning category. In addition to the base disinfectant brand, the current product lineup includes Lysol Toilet Bowl Cleaner for bathrooms; Lysol Deodorizing Cleaner for floors and large surfaces; Lysol Direct Cleaner, a direct-application convenience produce; and Lysol Pine Action Cleaner for consumers who prefer the scent and cleaning power of pine.

While each of these products has helped build the line, the brand's most successful line extension remains one of its earliest—Lysol Disinfectant Spray. This $100 million product is a curious hybrid. In addition to providing a convenient method of application, this aerosol product has taken the Lysol brand name into yet another home cleaning category—room deodorizing. To many consumers the product's distinctive smell connotes a purification that goes beyond mere air freshening.

In addition to the logical cleaning/disinfectant story, an enhanced emotional benefit was also a critical ingredient in Lysol's success. The original liquid disinfectant product had a strong clinical association. While the base product provided the important emotional benefit of security against disease, its image appeared harsh and unfriendly to some consumers. Realizing the limitations of this laboratory image, Lysol began to consciously evolve the product's emotional benefit from "cool" protection to a warmer, caring image.

As always, advertising was the means for accomplishing this transformation. In TV commercials today, Lysol products are always depicted in a friendly home setting. Children and babies are usually present. On an emotional level, the message is clear: parents who care use Lysol to keep their family's environment germfree. It is a powerful emotional communication and one that is relevant to all Lysol products.

On the strength of its expanded brand positioning, Lysol has eclipsed such established brand names as Mr. Clean, Spic & Span, and Pine Sol. Currently it enjoys a dominant position in the American home cleaning market.

Case Study 2: Jell-O

In the early 80s one of America's most venerable, established brand names found itself in a not so venerable position. While Jell-O, the perennial leader in the gelatin and pudding categories, held a commanding share in those markets, category sales were declining steeply and Jell-O sales were dropping right along with the rest.

Despite the best efforts of General Foods (GF) to update the Jell-O brands, traditional gelatins and puddings were increasingly perceived as old-fashioned products by many consumers. Because they required some preparation, they were also viewed as incompatible with the more harried life-styles of many working women. In short Jell-O was confronted with a classic marketing dilemma—holding a growing piece of a shrinking pie.

While the gelatin segment was shrinking, other segments of the dessert market were experiencing rapid growth. To maintain its long-term leadership position in the dessert business, GF determined that the Jell-O franchise had to expand into these growth areas. Frozen confectionery desserts were targeted as the best place to establish a Jell-O presence.

Having made the decision to expand, GF was confronted with another classic dilemma: how to maximize leverage and minimize consumer confusion when taking a brand name strongly associated with a particular product category and moving it to another category. In short the Jell-O brand positioning had to be expanded to accommodate a broader product line.

To accomplish this task, GF realized that the new entry could not stray too far from the brand's rational benefit—the great taste of Jell-O. Through the magic of R&D, the rational product benefit was transferred into a new medium—frozen pudding on a stick. The approach to naming was straightforward as well. To strengthen the linkage with the base brand, GF dubbed its new creation Jell-O Pudding Pops.

Great taste was only the rational half of the Jell-O product benefit. The brand provided an emotional benefit as well. Simply stated, Jell-O's emotional benefit was fun: kids had fun eating Jell-O, and parents had fun watching them eat it. To ensure the success of Pudding Pops in the frozen dessert category, GF knew the Jell-O "fun" benefit had to be enhanced in a way that was relevant to the new category.

Their solution made advertising history. Bill Cosby, a personality already associated with humor, was chosen to serve as the Pudding Pops spokesperson. In the introductory Pudding Pops commercials a delightful interplay was set up between Cosby and several very appealing children. Before long, Cosby and the kids became the personifications of the fun taste of Jell-O Pudding Pops and the communication of the brand's emotional benefit was enhanced.

The campaign was so successful that Cosby eventually became the spokesperson for the entire Jell-O line, bringing with him the strong kids/fun association from Pudding Pops. Pudding Pops went on to become an over $100 million business and a major new product success. In the process, Jell-O's product positioning was greatly expanded and the brand's overall share of the dessert market was significantly increased.

DEVELOPING THE LINE

Case Study 3: Crest

In the late 70s the Crest brand was riding high at Procter & Gamble. With a commanding 40 percent share of the toothpaste market, Crest enjoyed a wide lead over number-two Colgate, whose share hovered at about 20 percent. The brand's category dominance was so great it seemed impervious to competition. Nonetheless, over the next 10 years, the market situation changed dramatically and Crest was subjected to a serious challenge.

After years of reacting to market developments, number-two Colgate became aggressively proactive. In quick succession Colgate introduced a series of major line extensions, including a pump package and a new gel form. Although Crest eventually matched these entries, the brand was slow to respond. By the mid-80s Colgate was breathing down Crest's neck. Its share had risen to almost 30 percent, while Crest's had fallen to a similar level.

Responding to the intense competitive pressure, Crest management began to gear up its own product development activities. The first priority was to fill the competitive gaps in the Crest line by introducing both gel and pump products. Then the Crest brand group began to systematically identify and pursue other line extension opportunities. Before long they spotted their first big opening.

In the aging of the baby boom generation, America's most significant demographic group, P&G managers saw an opportunity for a major new product entry. Research showed that tartar buildup on teeth became a problem for most adults as they grew older. The Crest R&D group was given the assignment of developing a product that could alleviate this problem. When they were successful in identifying such an ingredient, Tartar Control Crest formula was born.

Tartar Control Crest formula was introduced in 1985, months ahead of a comparable Colgate product. By the end of the year, largely on the strength of Tartar Control volume, Crest had regained much of its former share. Since then Crest has maintained its new product momentum through the development and introduction of numerous aesthetic (new flavors), product form, and formula variations. What's more, the brand is slated to intensify its new product activity even further in the future.

According to *Advertising Age*,

> Procter & Gamble will forge ahead with what the company considers its most aggressive push since 1985 for Crest . . . . Crest Neat Squeeze, a squeezable soft pump, will roll out nationally . . . . P&G also plans to boost Crest's position as the leading toothpaste for children with a limited summertime promotion for Sparkle Crest fruit flavors in clear squeezable tubes. The flavors—Hawaiian Punch and Orange Bubblefun—will target kids ages 6 to 12.[1]

On top of all this, waiting in the wings is the brand's next blockbuster product, Ultra Protection Crest. Targeted for middle-aged adults, Ultra Protection is billed as the next-generation toothpaste. The product's antiplaque formula is reputed to help protect against gum disease. Originally scheduled for 1991 launch, Ultra Protection is now on a two-year hold while awaiting FDA new-drug approval.

Driven by an aggressive line development program, Crest's

market share had rebounded to 38 percent of the $1 billion market by the end of 1990. Having experienced first-hand the positive impact of a coordinated, offensive product development program, it is doubtful that Crest will return to its former passive mode in the foreseeable future.

Case Study 4: Coca-Cola

Few will ever forget Coca-Cola's decision in 1984 to improve its original formula. When the company announced the replacement of the classic Coke flavor with a new version, Americans reacted with shock and outrage. The public outcry was so intense that the company reneged on its decision within a matter of months. Rather than marketing new Coke as a product replacement, management finally decided to market it as a line extension.

Although the decision path in this instance was highly unorthodox, the ultimate outcome was extremely positive for Coke. In addition, this case provided some important lessons for all marketers about product line development. Unlike most consumer research, which is conducted in confidence and shared with only a select few, Coca-Cola inadvertently conducted their consumer research in the public marketplace, where the results were apparent to everyone.

Historically Coke had been very successful with its only major line extension, Diet Coke. After years of face-to-face competition with Diet Pepsi, Diet Coke was still the leading brand in this important segment. A later diet line extension, Caffeine Free Diet Coke, was also a significant hit. But Coke had stayed away from direct line extensions of the base brand, probably out of fear of creating consumer confusion and destabilizing the core business. Ironically this same caution did not extend to product improvements.

The decision to change the Coke formula was precipitated by mounting pressure from the brand's archcompetitor, Pepsi. Beginning in the mid-70s, the famous "Pepsi Challenge" campaign graphically depicted consumers preferring the taste of Pepsi over Coke on a blind, unidentified basis. By all accounts the Pepsi Challenge gave the Pepsi business a major boost. Equally disturbing was the fact that these commercials highlighted a disturbing trend that Coke had discovered in its own research—a sizable percentage of consumers liked Pepsi better.

In retrospect, what Coke's research really pointed to was a major product development opportunity for the Coke line. It was not that all Coke drinkers were asking for a product change, only some of them were. For the most part these restless drinkers tended to be younger consumers who preferred a higher level of sweetness.

In hindsight, there was absolutely no need to put the franchise at risk by changing the base-brand formula. As history has shown, a line extension could appeal very effectively to Pepsi-prone consumers while the base brand could continue unaffected. When the original formula was reintroduced as Coke Classic, the public heaved a collective sigh of relief and the Coke franchise grew at a faster rate than it had in several years.

In an era of line extensions, it is impossible for one product, even Coke, to appeal to everyone. As such it is not only desirable but necessary to grow the line through multiple line extensions. As a result of the public's initial rejection of new Coke, Coca-Cola was dragged, kicking and screaming, out of the age of mass marketing and into the age of micromarketing. Once there the company discovered that the massive size of the Coke franchise could easily support other new line extensions.

After bringing back Coke Classic, Coke next introduced cherry Coke, a line extension clearly targeted at the teenage end of the market. More recently a caffeine-free version of Coke Classic was launched. When combined with new Coke, industry sources estimate that the two line extensions have added approximately 4 share points to the Coke line. In a $45 billion category where every share point is worth $450 million, this gain is substantial to say the least.

LEVERAGING THE SPENDING

Case Study 5: Campbell's Soup

A recent report by *Advertising Age* revealed two remarkable statistics about Campbell's soup:

1. In 1989 the Campbell's line recorded total sales of $1.3 billion.
2. In the same year, the line registered total media expenditures of $24 million.[2]

What is most remarkable about these statistics is that Campbell's was able to dominate the U.S. soup market with an advertising to sales ratio of less than 2 percent.

While megabrand status brings with it many competitive advantages, none is more devastating to smaller competitors than the marketing spending leverage that size bestows. This spending advantage is most apparent in the area of consumer advertising.

For example, while Campbell's invested less than 2 percent of 1990 sales in advertising, its share of category media spending was more than 50 percent. Smaller brands such as Knorr had to spend a much larger percentage of sales revenue on advertising to achieve a much smaller share.

With substantially larger media budgets, Campbell's is able to provide competitive levels of media support for each of its major line items and, at the same time, realize great flexibility in terms of spending tactics. With revenue generated by the sales of mature products, Campbell's shifted a portion of its ad dollars from older items to newer entries to help these products maximize their volume. In particular, Campbell's placed major advertising support behind the following line items:

1990 Media Expenditures ($ millions)

Red & white label	28.7
Chunky	11.0
Home Cookin'	8.6
Special Request	2.2
Microwaveable products	2.5

Source: Leading National Advertisers (LNA)

On the basis of sales alone, it is unlikely that either the low-sodium Special Request line or the new microwaveable products would have generated this level of media spending. However, both are considered growth opportunities for Campbell's and are worthy of investment spending.

In addition to flexibility, a megabrand like Campbell's enjoys other advertising advantages over smaller brands. For example, Campbell's benefits from an extremely high preexisting level of brand awareness. To duplicate this top-of-mind awareness, a competitor would have to invest countless millions of dollars. Obviously it costs Campbell's far less to simply maintain it.

Then there is the halo effect of advertising itself. While the specifics may vary, the fundamental message in all Campbell's communications is the brand's theme, "Soup is good food." Ads for any item in the Campbell's line subtly reinforce each other. In addition, *all* the brand's advertising generates awareness of the Campbell's brand name.

As a result of its dominant market position, Campbell's has incredible advertising and marketing spending leverage. Because of this, it is virtually impossible for any competitor to challenge the brand head-on.

Case Study 6: Clorox Bleach

In most of America's 65 million households, laundry is done at least twice a week. Each time, at least one laundry load contains all white garments. In more than half of these washloads when liquid bleach is added, the bleach that accompanies the detergent is Clorox liquid bleach.

Few companies have been as successful with any business as Clorox has been with its flagship bleach brand. Since its introduction in 1916, Clorox liquid bleach has been the leading product in the liquid bleach category. The familiar white bottle can be found in the laundry rooms of millions of American homes.

Like all megabrands, Clorox enjoys tremendous marketing leverage. Since the brand has only one significant national competitor (Purex), Clorox is able to maintain its position of leadership in the $500 million liquid bleach category with great spending efficiencies. In keeping with the principles of megabrand marketing, this leverage is particularly pronounced in consumer advertising.

According to published sources, Clorox liquid bleach media expenditures increased modestly over the three-year period 1987–89, as follows:

Clorox Bleach Media Spending ($ millions)

1987	8.8
1988	9.5
1989	11.6

Source: LNA

On an absolute dollar basis, these media expenditures are highly efficient and very low for the leading brand in a major consumer category. They are even lower when considered as a percentage of total brand sales, yet during this time period Clorox successfully introduced two major line extensions. By boldly placing much of the line's media spending behind these new products, Clorox was able to aggressively leverage these businesses, with minimal negative impact on the existing base brand.

In 1987 Clorox launched the first of these products: Fresh Scent Clorox, an aesthetic line extension developed to provide a scent alternative to the traditional product. The basic formula is identical to regular Clorox. Actual product performance is also the same. These facts were clearly communicated in the introductory ad copy: "The strength of Clorox in a great new scent."

Based on positive consumer response, Clorox decided to place much of the regular Clorox liquid bleach media spending behind Fresh Scent in an effort to maximize the new entry's awareness and trial. This decision paid off handsomely. Not only was the Fresh Scent launch a major success in its own right, but the overall Clorox business also increased.

Encouraged by consumers' interest in scented products, Clorox moved quickly to maintain the momentum. In 1989 the company introduced a second scented line extension—Lemon Fresh Clorox. Once again Clorox decided to reconfigure its media spending. This time the company was even more aggressive. As illustrated by the table below, Clorox decided to eliminate virtually all support behind the base product and place the spending behind the two scented line extensions:

Clorox Bleach Media Spending ($ millions)

	1987	1988	1989
Regular Clorox	5.2	6.1	.2
Fresh Scent	3.6	3.4	6.1
Lemon Fresh	—	—	5.3

Source: LNA

Once again the decision paid off. Lemon Fresh Clorox grew to become an even greater success than Fresh Scent. Together the two line extensions increased the overall Clorox market share. Clorox was able to realize tremendous spending leverage because the basic benefit of all its bleaches was identical—whitening and brightening. As such, all Clorox advertising, whether for Regular, Fresh Scent, or Lemon Fresh, was a vehicle for building brand awareness and reinforcing the Clorox liquid bleach cleaning story. What a marvelous synergy!

EXECUTING THE PLAN

Case Study 7: Tide

No product line is more representative of the demassification of the U.S. consumer market than Tide, America's number-one brand of laundry detergent. Over the past three years, Tide has introduced a series of line extensions that have progressively strengthened the brand's leadership position. Without question, a dynamic product development program has been a key contributor to Tide's continued success. However, equally important has been Procter & Gamble's (P&G's) skill at executing a complex, multilayered marketing plan with great precision and accuracy.

Tide's growing product line is living proof that the detergent category today is no longer a single mass market but a mass of smaller markets. Building off the established base of Tide powder and liquid, P&G introduced three new line extensions targeted at newly identified market segments:

1. Unscented Tide—Perfume-free variations of Tide powder and liquid targeted at allergy sufferers.
2. Tide with Bleach—Powder detergent with color-safe bleach targeted at consumers seeking a convenient, effective, one-step cleaning system.
3. Ultra Tide—A superconcentrated form of Tide powder in a small box targeted at environmentally conscious consumers.

To maximize the effectiveness of Tide's micromarketing approach, P&G has shifted away from the traditional mass medium of network TV. The company has started to rely more heavily on more targeted media, such as spot TV, cable TV, and print, to reach individual user groups. This shift in media strategy is reflected in the media spending pattern of Tide with Bleach during its introductory year:

Tide with Bleach 1990 Media Spending

	($ millions)	% of Total
Network TV	8.0	49
Spot TV	3.5	21
Cable TV	2.2	13
Print	2.8	17

Source: LNA

P&G has also begun to acknowledge the ethnic diversity of its consumers by investing more heavily in Hispanic media. According to industry sources, the Tide line spent $5 million in Hispanic television during 1990.[3] In addition, the brand produces variations of all of its commercials using black actors, obviously targeted for the black market.

Tactically speaking, Tide is becoming increasingly proficient at executing a complex, tiered plan. On the media front the brand supports each major line entry with a separate advertising campaign. To kick off a major new product launch such as Tide with Bleach, the brand will shift much of its advertising away from established products to the new product. Once spending has returned to sustaining levels, advertising synergy is created through the use of a common testimonial format across all line entries and a common theme line, "When it's got to be clean, it's got to be Tide."

In the area of promotion, all Tide products engage in heavy consumer couponing. They also supplement this activity with joint promotions with other Tide and P&G products to gain greater spending efficiency.

As a result of successful product development and a well-executed marketing plan, the Tide line registered supermarket sales of $970 million in 1989.[4] Tide enjoyed a substantial volume increase, while the overall detergent market underwent a significant decline.

Case Study 8: Tylenol

Few megabrands have been exposed to the kind of marketplace adversity that afflicted the Tylenol franchise in the early 1980s, when it was struck by the devastating product tampering scandal. Despite this tragic incident and the subsequent competitive challenge posed by the introduction of a whole new class of pain relievers (Advil and Nuprin), Tylenol has managed to withstand all threats and remain atop the multibillion dollar over-the-counter (OTC) analgesic category.

Tylenol's enduring strength can be traced to its strong association with doctors and hospitals. Tylenol is not unique among OTC drug brands in emphasizing its professional heritage. However, it has been more successful than other brands in maintaining a professional franchise while aggressively promoting its products to consumers. Tylenol's exceptional success with both of these key target groups is the result of a finely executed marketing plan that simultaneously targets doctors, hospitals, and consumers through synergistic, complementary programs.

In micromarketing the Tylenol line, Johnson & Johnson appeals to its professional and consumer audiences with different product mixes, sold through separate sales organizations and supported by distinct marketing communications programs. The focus of Tylenol's professional marketing efforts is a prescription entry—Tylenol with codeine. Tylenol is unique among the major OTC analgesic brands in having a prescription product that is available only through physicians. The presence of a prescription

Tylenol product has allowed J&J to preserve strong physician allegiance in the face of a massive consumer promotion, which can often dilute a brand's professional support.

To promote Tylenol to the medical profession, the McNeil Laboratories Division of Johnson & Johnson maintains a separate sales organization. This group makes hundreds of thousands of calls per year on doctors and hospitals detailing the advantages of Tylenol with codeine and the rest of the Tylenol line. As a result of ongoing promotion, professional loyalty to the Tylenol franchise remains very strong. In fact Tylenol with codeine is the most frequently prescribed pain reliever among doctors today.

In addition to generating a major business in its own right, the brand's ongoing medical activities also provide the bedrock for its consumer marketing program. From the beginning Tylenol's consumer advertising has stressed the brand's doctor and hospital heritage (e.g., "Hospitals recommend Tylenol more than all other pain relievers combined."). This mass media message, repeated at high levels over the years, combined with frequent doctor and hospital recommendations creates a highly professional and persuasive image for the brand. In fact Tylenol's medical endorsements reinforced through consumer advertising have created such an aura around the brand that it is often described by competitors as being "in a class by itself."

In addition to the rub-off from its professional marketing program, Tylenol was able to create further synergy with its consumer marketing program. Over the years the brand has been very successful at extending its basic analgesic franchise. By 1990 the line included regular-strength and extra-strength products sold in a variety of tablet and capsule forms. However, J&J has managed to build this supersuccessful, $600 million line by placing *all* advertising support behind the extra-strength product.

To date, the halo effect of Extra-Strength Tylenol advertising has effectively supported the regular-strength product as well. In addition, Extra-Strength Tylenol advertising has provided a significant brand name awareness boost for other advertised Tylenol line extensions in related categories. Through skillful execution and coordination of its consumer and professional marketing programs, Tylenol has been able to stave off strong competitors and maintain its dominance in the lucrative OTC analgesic market.

MEGAFLOPS

SQUANDERING THE SPENDING

Case Study 9: Alka-Seltzer

Throughout the 1960s Alka-Seltzer rode atop the U.S. antacid market. Not only did the brand enjoy the number-one market position, its highly creative advertising campaigns had put the Alka-Seltzer brand name top-of-mind with American consumers. Tag lines from popular Alka-Seltzer commercials, such as "Try it, you'll like it!" and "I can't believe I ate the whole thing!" became a part of the everyday vernacular.

But as the 70s began, Alka-Seltzer's leadership position began to decline. Shifts within the antacid market were placing the franchise at serious risk. Traditionally the antacid category had been divided into three major segments: effervescents, chewable tablets, and liquids. The problem was that Alka-Seltzer's segment—effervescents—was dropping in terms of consumer popularity, while tablets and liquids were on the rise.

At Miles Laboratories, management recognized the problem and correctly concluded that Alka-Seltzer's positioning had to be expanded beyond the effervescent segment. An aggressive product development program was initiated to create Alka-Seltzer line extensions for the tablet and liquid segments. The first product to emerge from the pipeline was a chewable antacid called Alka-2. After performing well in test markets, Alka-2 was introduced nationally in 1975.

While Alka-2 was a superior product in taste and texture, it was up against a tough, entrenched competitor in Warner-Lambert's Rolaids. Predictably Rolaids reacted to the Alka-2 introduction by dramatically increasing its promotion and advertising expenditures. The goal behind this increased spending was to make the cost of entry into the chewable segment prohibitively expensive for Miles.

Warner-Lambert also used another trump card in its battle with Miles. Unlike the effervescent segment, a large percentage of chewable sales took place at supermarket checkout counters and confectionery stands. The Warner-Lambert sales force had been put together to effectively service these distribution outlets; the

Miles sales force had not. To further blunt the Alka-2 entry, Warner-Lambert stepped up its retail activities towards these trade classes.

As a result of the Rolaids program, Alka-2's growth was slowed appreciably and Miles Laboratories was confronted with a difficult decision. They could spend what was required to establish the product or resign themselves to a lower market share—knowing that a lower share might not be large enough to sustain the business long-term. If they chose further investment, the obvious source of funds would be Alka-Seltzer itself.

Fearful of exposing the base brand, Miles opted for the conservative approach and maintained Alka-Seltzer spending. By the end of the decade, Alka-2 had virtually disappeared from store shelves. With the benefit of 20/20 hindsight, it is apparent that the decision should have been just the opposite. By diverting large-scale support from the base brand, the entire franchise could have been strengthened!

At the time of the Alka-2 introduction, Alka-Seltzer had no direct competition. What's more, its consumer awareness was extremely high. The brand could have carried on for a year or longer with greatly reduced marketing activities. The savings could have been used to increase Alka-2's advertising and promotional programs and strengthen the capabilities of the Miles sales organization.

But, alas, this did not happen. The Alka-Seltzer brand remained mired in a declining segment. Chastened by the Alka-2 experience, the company turned down its antacid development activities. By 1990 Alka-Seltzer had dropped from first to fifth in the U.S. antacid market.

CONFUSING BRAND POSITIONING

Case Study 10: Ban Antiperspirant

In the mid-70s the Ban antiperspirant business was booming at Bristol-Myers. The centerpiece of the line, Ban Roll-on, had grown rapidly from a secondary market position to become the number-one antiperspirant in unit sales. The brand's dynamic growth was stimulated by an effective, comparative advertising campaign and a burst of negative publicity regarding aerosol sprays.

A few years earlier Ban had broken an advertising campaign built around the scientific fact that a roll-on antiperspirant is more effective at stopping wetness than an aerosol spray because of its method of direct application. In the new campaign Ban compared itself directly to the leading aerosol brands and highlighted its superior efficacy. Consumers were receptive to the head-to-head comparisons and Ban's market share began to rise steadily.

At about the same time, a number of scientific reports were published linking the fluorocarbon propellants in aerosol sprays to ozone depletion. Responding to a government mandate, spray manufacturers were forced to reformulate their products and replace the fluorocarbon propellants with a less dangerous hydrocarbon variety. Consumers' concerns about the environment and dissatisfactions with the reformulated sprays gave a further boost to the roll-on business. Clearly Ban was a product in the right place at the right time.

The product line was also at a crossroads. Prior to the fluorocarbon controversy, Bristol-Myers had been focusing its product development efforts on another direct-application segment of the antiperspirant market—sticks—and was in the process of test marketing a Ban stick product. Sensing the vulnerability of the spray segment, Bristol-Myers abandoned its well-conceived product development program and shifted its emphasis from sticks to the development of a nonaerosol, pump spray product. Working on a "crash" timetable, the product was introduced as Ban Basic in 1976.

Ban Basic proved to be a disastrous change in direction for the Ban line for two reasons. First, consumers did not perceive a pump spray product to be an acceptable replacement for an aerosol spray. Second, the launch of Ban Basic diverted the brand's attention from the real growth opportunity—the stick segment. After two years of launch and relaunch, Ban Basic failed to maintain a significant share.

Meanwhile, another competitor, Mennen, began to wake up to the growth potential in sticks. The number-one stick brand, Speed Stick, was a Mennen product and the company began to step up its marketing activity. By the time Bristol-Myers refocused its attention on sticks, Mennen had further solidified its leadership position in this segment. During the time of the pump spray diversion, the window of opportunity was closing for Ban in the stick business.

The Ban Basic foray hurt the brand in another important respect. Ban had built its business on the strength of head-to-head comparisons of its roll-on (direct application) versus competitive sprays (indirect application). Now suddenly, with Ban Basic, the brand was selling its own spray product. These seemingly contradictory messages were confusing to many consumers.

Today Ban remains a major player in the antiperspirant category. However, the brand's opportunity to transform itself into a megabrand seems to have been permanently lost.

REALIZING THE POTENTIAL

As these case histories show, the power of a megabrand line is immense in today's marketplace. By the same token the stature of these brands does not automatically guarantee continued success. Through ineffective marketing and management, it is still possible for megabrands to lose their advantage and fail to achieve their long-term goals. To realize their full potential and maintain their leadership positions, megabrands must operate according to clearly defined principles and disciplines. In particular they must:

1. Expand brand positioning through aggressive line extensions.
2. Continuously fill existing gaps in the line and develop new items.
3. Leverage their advertising and promotion spending to support new entries.
4. Creatively execute the entire marketing plan.

When they follow these principles, the scope of their market dominance can be truly extraordinary.

NOTES

1. Jennifer Lawrence, "Big Crest for P&G," *Advertising Age*, February 25, 1991, p. 10.
2. "Powerful Brand 'Families' Key to Growth," *Superbrands 1990*, supplement to *Adweek*, p. 148.
3. "Adding Still More to an Industry on the Verge of Gridlock," *Superbrands 1990*, supplement to *Adweek*, p. 156.
4. Ibid.
5. "The OTC Industry Embraces the Newly Converted," *Superbrands 1990*, supplement to *Adweek*, p. 168.

PART 3

TAKING ON THE MEGABRANDS BY NICHE MARKETING

Chapter Nine

Developing Niche Products: A New Approach

As the power of the megabrands continues to grow, the task confronting smaller competitors can, at times, appear overwhelming. How can their brands possibly compete against market dominators with massive marketing budgets? How can their product development programs succeed against competitive efforts backed by unlimited financial resources? When they develop viable new products, how can they afford to introduce them with the costs of market entry rising into the stratosphere?

Without a doubt the challenges confronting smaller products today are considerable—but far from insoluble. Significant opportunities that are potentially quite profitable persist in the marketplace. Inherent in the very strengths of the megabrands are weaknesses that can be exploited by agile marketers. However, to take advantage of these opportunities, companies must be willing to make a radical break with the traditions of the past.

Before their actions can change, companies must change their thinking. They must be willing to move away from time-worn formulas and to define problems and opportunities in new ways. To succeed against mammoth competitors, they cannot continue to approach tough issues from the same, time-worn perspectives. Instead they must develop a new mind-set. Consistent with that mind-set, they must take the leap and abandon many traditional business approaches and practices in favor of unfamiliar but dynamic new programs.

CIRCUMVENTING MEGABRAND STRENGTHS

In short, smaller brands can never expect to win by following the rules of their larger opponents. To prevail against large competitors, managers of smaller products must have the vision and courage to create a new set of rules. Rather than playing to a megabrand's strengths, they must find ways to circumvent those strengths. Instead of mimicking megabrand strategies, they must invent new strategies to keep their larger competitors off-balance and at a safe distance. Otherwise they will find themselves in a perpetual mismatch, forever outspent, outplayed, and ultimately outplaced.

Recently a new strategy has begun to emerge for dealing with the megabrand challenge. Known as *niche marketing*, the strategy suggests that a brand can most readily protect itself from the onslaught of the giants by narrowing its focus and concentrating on a small portion of a market segment, or niche. By becoming superspecialized, the niche product can satisfy the needs of this smaller segment more effectively than a more broadly based brand. Drawing on a biological model, the principle suggests that just as small creatures can survive in nature by finding a small niche, so smaller brands can survive in the marketplace by doing the same.

NICHE MARKETING: CONVENTIONAL WISDOM

In a recent article, marketing consultant Gerald A. Michaelson provided a familiar definition of niche marketing. According to Michaelson,

Niche marketing [is] finding small groups of consumers who can be served within a segment. . . . The more tightly you focus your concentration, the more sure you are to own the segment. The broader the segment, the greater the risk that you will share the segment with someone else. . . . The key issues are concentrating on a clearly identified target market, then finding a relative superiority which gives you a competitive advantage.[1]

As defined by this popular vision, niche marketing is at best an attractive technique for building and protecting a small business. At worst it represents a defensive, bunker-mentality approach to consumer products marketing. In either case it is hardly the aggressive strategy that most managers require to prosper and grow in the face of the megabrands.

If the potential of niche marketing were truly described by this popular notion, the overall impact of niche products in the marketplace would be marginal at best. From the perspective of the megabrands, niche products would represent about as much of a competitive threat as gnats to an elephant. As such, smaller companies would have to look elsewhere for a viable growth strategy.

Fortunately this conventional definition does not begin to describe niche marketing's true potential. Conventional thinkers who cling to this traditional definition have taken the concept of segmentation too literally. While they are right about one thing— specialization is the essence of niche marketing—this specialization need not be narrow. It need not restrict a product to a minor category position.

NICHE MARKETING: NEW WISDOM

While many large corporations are caught up in the conventional thinking about niche marketing, some leading-edge companies have begun to grasp the larger meaning of segment specialization. Their success in this area is leading to a new, nontraditional understanding of niche marketing, one that is more expansive and proactive. Using this expanded definition,

A niche product is characterized by the extreme specialization of some segment (aspect) of its marketing program. Not only does

this specialization provide defense and insulation from category competitors, it can also serve as a platform for aggressive expansion into the category at large and the achievement of significant market share.

This enhanced definition differs from the traditional description of niche products in three respects. Most importantly it proclaims that a niche product's specialization no longer has to be understood exclusively in terms of product positioning. Naturally there will continue to be some niche products defined in this manner. However, a niche product's specialization can also be conceived in terms of other aspects of its marketing program (e.g., pricing or distribution). These alternative forms of specialization may well provide the greatest long-term volume opportunities.

Second, when broadly defined, a niche product's specialization not only creates a barrier against competitive attack but can also serve as a platform for aggressive expansion. Once established, the product can begin to carefully move away from its specialization and enter the general market. For example, once firmly established in its home area, a regional food product can begin to roll out to the rest of the country. Even after it has moved on, a product's heritage of specialization continues to represent a key point of difference versus competitive brands.

Finally there is the matter of timing. In most cases, a niche product's specialization does not materialize overnight. It takes time to develop, often several years. Consequently, its developmental time frame is more extended than that of more broadly based products. Most niche products do not spring full-blown from the minds of product managers. They evolve in the market. Once developed, they have great permanence.

DEVELOPING NICHE PRODUCTS

To successfully differentiate their products, niche marketers must create a competitive advantage through the extreme specialization of some aspect of the product's marketing program. Over the years this specialization has tended to fall into four general areas:

1. Focused product positioning.
2. Regional marketing.

3. Exclusive channels of distribution.

4. Value pricing.

Not surprisingly the niche marketing efforts of major corporations have often focused on product positioning. For examples of other types of niche marketing success, one must often look to smaller companies and start-up, entrepreneurial operations. However, regardless of approach or place of origin, all niche marketing successes share a common characteristic: they represent a break with traditional mass marketing thinking. In fact the lingering mass market mentality that persists in most large companies creates the basic opportunities for niche marketing innovations.

Successful niche marketers usually have another quality in common: agility. Often they are the first to identify the niche opportunity. In niche marketing timing is everything. While major market segments may be large enough to comfortably accommodate more than one competitor, marketing niches seldom are. To borrow from an old army saying, "There are only two kinds of niche marketers: the quick and the dead!"

Focused Product Positioning

Advertising executive Laurel Cutler, vice chairperson of FCB/Leber Katz Partners in New York, is known throughout the industry as an astute forecaster of social and business trends. In discussing the qualities that will characterize successful enterprises in the 1990s, she observed, "There is no future for products everybody likes a little. Only for products somebody likes a lot."[2] According to Cutler, products that "somebody likes a lot" have "intensity." One way niche products can achieve this intensity is through a focused product positioning.

When precisely focused, niche products can achieve greater intensity than line extensions of major brands because they are conceived and brought to the market solely to satisfy a specialized consumer need. In a sense they are born on the other side of the tracks from their major-brand counterparts and possess a more singular outlook on life.

Even today, the most successful and enlightened megabrand marketers still owe their philosophical allegiance to mass marketing. Their fundamental marketing strategy has been aptly described as mass customization. Their goal is to build a macro business through micromarketing of customized line extensions. Of necessity they must simultaneously keep a foot in both the macro and micro worlds.

As previously discussed, a megabrand is an extended line of products built off a common positioning that offers consumers variations of a common core benefit. Because a megabrand line is held together by a common positioning and core benefit, there is a built-in limit to how specialized any line item can become without severing its strategic links to the rest of the line. Since consumers must be able to perceive the benefits of the various megabrand line items as different but similar, a megabrand's need for *strategic continuity* within its line creates positioning opportunities for niche marketers.

Since niche products are not part of an extended product line, they are free to position themselves directly against a business opportunity. As a result their focus can be sharp and directed. Because they stand alone, they are also free to describe their product benefit in the most concise language appropriate to the particular situation. Niche products do not have to express their product benefit as a variation of an existing benefit; they can express it as a completely new benefit.

For example, back in the late 1970s, the Clorox company perceived a niche opportunity in the bathroom cleaning market. Bathroom mildew was a nagging problem that no brand had addressed directly. While many bathroom cleaners removed mildew from tile surfaces, existing products chose to define their core benefits more broadly as cleaning and disinfecting. By developing Tilex, a niche product designed to remove mildew stains, Clorox provided a more convincing solution to this problem for consumers.

Murphy's Oil Soap is another example from the home cleaning category of a successful niche brand with a focused product positioning. In the late 1980s, Murphy's Oil Soap began to appear on store shelves throughout the nation. While other brands were selling more general cleaning benefits, Murphy's positioned itself exclusively for use on wood surfaces. The idea caught on. Because of its focused positioning, Murphy's was able to establish a thriving, new niche in a mature and crowded market.

Interestingly, neither Tilex nor Murphy's could be considered a technological breakthrough. Both formulas could have been easily duplicated by a major competitor. But because these products got to the market first with a clear focus, consumers perceived them as special. Their focused positionings bestowed added credibility on the products. Once introduced, many consumers were unwilling to believe that a major brand line extension could perform as well as these specialty items.

Finally, it is instructive to consider the story of a niche product that walked away from a focused positioning and is now struggling to win it back. In 1982 a popular French soft drink called Orelia made its appearance in the U.S. marketplace. As *Forbes* magazine stated, "They [the manufacturer] had modest— and, as it turned out, realistic—ambitions for the drink. . . . The idea was to win a place in the trendy, premium-priced beverage niche in which Perrier and flavored seltzers held sway."[3]

Initially Orelia met its goals. However, in 1985 the brand was acquired by another French company with a much bigger objective—a 1 percent share of the massive U.S. soft drink market. The new owner changed the name to Orangina and launched a broad-scale consumer advertising campaign. Unfortunately the product was outspent and outmarketed by several major soft drink competitors who knew the market cold. Despite heavy spending, the repositioning was a disaster.

According to *Forbes*, "After four years in the mass market, Orangina had only a minuscule share of the orange soda segment and had lost an estimated $15 million. Pernod Ricard has not withdrawn Orangina from the U.S. shelves. But it is retreating to the trendy drink niche it probably should have tried to fill in the first place."[4]

Like many American marketers before them, the French discovered with Orangina that when it comes to niche marketing, more is very often less.

Regional Marketing

As discussed earlier, a niche product is defined by the extreme specialization of some aspect of its marketing program. Beyond product positioning, this specialization can be provided by an exclusive concentration in just one region of the country. It is important to distinguish between true regional marketing and decentralized marketing. A regional marketer sells a product *only* in a specific region; a decentralized marketer sells a product nationally, utilizing different marketing approaches in different parts of the country.

Since the vast majority of national corporations take a national marketing approach, the best examples of regional niche marketing successes are usually found in smaller regional companies. In fact there appears to be an established pattern of major companies acquiring successful regional marketers, then rolling their products out to the rest of the country. Once in national distribution, such products continue to stress their regional roots. It is these regional characteristics that afford these products their distinct character.

Interestingly the regional roots of many of America's largest brands are still reflected in the share patterns across the country. According to marketing consultant Thomas Osborne,

> National markets are statistics, summaries of individual local and regional markets. Many of our most familiar brands get 40 to 80 percent of their volume from a "core" region and are primarily a specialty brand in the rest of the country. It is a rare product category that enjoys a semblance of uniform consumption across the country, nor do a majority of brands within a category have anything like a uniform brand share.[5]

Regional niche products span all categories from insecticides to allergy medications. However, since culinary tastes are often regional, the food and beverage category provides some of the most illustrative examples of successful regional niche marketing. For example, about 10 years ago a Kansas City psychologist developed his own brand of barbecue sauce and began to market it locally. He called his concoction K.C. Masterpiece. Before long K.C. Masterpiece had surpassed the national brands of barbecue sauce and became the local category leader. Then in 1988, Clorox acquired K.C. Masterpiece and rolled it out across the nation. Today it is the number-two barbecue sauce brand nationwide.

The California Market

Over the years California has provided many examples of successful regional niche marketing. One of the most flamboyant was California Cooler, the country's first wine cooler. Introduced in California in the early 1980s by two young entrepreneurs, the product quickly became a statewide rage. Soon after, California Cooler was acquired by Brown Forman and introduced nationally. Although the product had a relatively brief life cycle, it performed very well for a few years across the country and spawned numerous imitators.

Many experts believe that California continues to offer numerous opportunities for regional niche marketing. According to Osborne,

> Very few manufacturers are developing marketing plans or product line extensions just for California. The nation beckons and the economics of national distribution and media discounts are seductive. Yet California's 26 million affluent consumers are worth special attention; they certainly offer enough potential to justify a separate marketing and production effort. A clear focus on California could help lift many also-ran, designed-for-the-national-average, parity consumer products to success, at the very least in that one very rewarding market. The Texas or New England markets would also be worth a fresh start and a new operating focus that does not depend necessarily on what is done in California or anywhere else. A resulting portfolio of California-style, Texas-style, and New England-style products could be very attractive.[6]

Whether in California or other local areas, regional niche marketing is a viable marketing option. To succeed, every brand does not have to become a national brand. In fact the focus and specialization of a regional marketing effort can provide major competitive advantages over larger, national adversaries.

Exclusive Channels of Distribution

Historically marketers of major consumer product lines have sold their brands through three mass distribution outlets: food stores, drug stores, and mass merchandisers. Their sales and marketing organizations often assume that these outlets must always be part of the distribution mix. As such, this assumption has shaped the overall conduct of the business.

While three-outlet distribution remains the ultimate objective of traditional brand management, this goal may not be attainable in all cases. What's more, it may not be preferable. It may be far more desirable to niche market a brand exclusively in a single distribution channel for an extended period of time before introducing it more broadly. In this way, a specialized identity can be created for the product that can differentiate it from the competition. The brand's exclusive distribution channel may be one of the three major outlets or it may not.

The beauty aids industry has provided many prominent examples of successful distribution niche marketing. For example, many of America's leading hair-care products got their start as products sold exclusively through hair salons. Clairol, Vidal Sassoon, Jhirmack, and others share this common heritage.

Not only did the salon distribution approach provide these brands with protection against larger competitors, it also brought with it the explicit or implicit endorsement of the hair-care professional. This endorsement lent these products greater credibility and resulted in significant competitive differentiation in what were often parity markets. Finally it created a rock-solid foundation for eventual expansion into more traditional distribution outlets.

Obviously to duplicate the niche distribution successes of a Clairol or Sassoon, major packaged goods manufacturers would have to break the established mold and begin calling on an entirely new class of trade. In cases where the existing sales organization was not operating at full efficiency, sales personnel could be retrained to perform this task; in cases where the organization was functioning at maximum capacity, a specialized salon group could be established. Under either scenario, it would require departing from familiar, established business practices.

Today, as a growing percentage of the salon business is concentrated with national chains, the effectiveness of a salon sales group could be substantial. All it would require is a different mind-set and a willingness to try something new. But of course, these kinds of changes are more easily said than done.

Within the consumer health-care market, there are comparable distribution niche marketing successes. Some of America's most prominent over-the-counter drug brands began their careers as distribution niche products with no consumer advertising. Rather than going directly to consumers, these products were promoted exclusively to pharmacists and physicians and distributed only in drug outlets. In place of traditional, direct-to-consumer advertising and promotion, the endorsements of health care professionals were used to build the business.

This strategy has repeatedly enjoyed remarkable success. For the physician or pharmacist, the benefit lies in being able to recommend to their patients a non-prescription product that is exclusively their own, thereby enhancing consumers' perceptions of their expert status. For the marketer, professional endorsement provides a powerful advantage that distinguishes a product from the competition and actually strengthens consumers' perceptions of product performance. Over the years research has shown that consumers are more loyal to and satisfied with products recommended by their doctor or pharmacist than with products promoted exclusively through the mass media.

The list of major OTC products built through distribution niche marketing includes many of the industry's most successful brands. Among these are such prominent names as Johnson & Johnson's Tylenol, Burroughs-Wellcome's Sudafed and Actifed cold medications, G.D. Searle's Metamucil laxative, Bristol-Myers' Keri Lotion, and Schering-Plough's Maalox antacid and Afrin nasal spray.

Once again, success required an extreme specialization. Without exception all of these products were originally sold by a highly trained, professional sales organization. Today niche marketing through drug outlets remains a viable model for marketing success. Companies seeking to break into this arena have the choice of building their own professional sales groups or seeking a co-marketing agreement with another corporation that has a functioning professional sales organization. Both approaches are eminently "doable" once the decision has been made to break with traditional procedures.

Another example of niche marketing success achieved through a specialized channel of distribution is Hill's Science Diet dog food. For years, Science Diet was sold exclusively through veterinarians' offices. While the brand offered an excellent, nutritionally balanced product line, it was Science Diet's strong vet association that gave it a state-of-the-art image. Recently Hill's was acquired by Colgate. Today the brand has expanded its distribution into mass outlets and initiated its first consumer advertising campaign.

Finally, direct-mail catalogs represent an alternate, exclusive distribution channel that has been used with resounding success by numerous companies over the years, but largely ignored by large consumer product marketers. While catalog marketing is too complex a subject to be covered in depth here, it is important to note that several leading packaged goods marketers, such as Kraft/General Foods and Campbell's, have begun to experiment with this distribution channel to market specialized product lines.

Compared to traditional distribution outlets, catalogs offer marketers many advantages, including the ability to customize products for individual consumers and efficiently manage inventories via a central location. In view of these pluses, catalogs represent a niche marketing distribution channel that will be utilized much more pervasively by major marketing companies in the future.

Value Pricing

As the battle against the megabrands continues to rage, value pricing is emerging as one of the most effective niche marketing approaches. Already considered one of the most persuasive selling techniques, the message of equivalent value at a lower cost is likely to become even more powerful during the decade of the 1990s. As real family income continues to shrink throughout the United States, consumers will grow even more receptive to the value pricing story.

This is not to suggest that corporations should rush headlong into the generic products business or become commodity suppliers for major store brands. Along the price/value continuum, generics will always command the pure price positioning, with store brands claiming the middle ground. The opportunity for a select group of branded products lies at the high end of the price/ value continuum. For these products the primary source of increased volume will not be the other price competitors already mentioned, but major branded products—including megabrands.

At first glance, a price/value positioning seems to present an insolvable paradox to major brand marketers because it appears to call for three contradictory results to be achieved simultaneously. These results are:

1. Effectively communicate the value pricing story to consumers through advertising and promotion.

2. Maintain a quality product at a low price.
3. Deliver an acceptable profit to the corporation.

In order to accomplish this seemingly impossible task, one condition is an absolute prerequisite: an established, high level of brand awareness.

Today it is next to impossible to successfully introduce a completely new value-priced brand. Short of voodoo economics, the financials simply do not add up. In today's mature markets, the price/value positioning is only viable for well-established brands that can trade off the awareness and consumer equity built through years of marketing spending. For these types of older products, a value pricing approach can represent a veritable fountain of youth. Not only can it create a protected market niche that is very difficult for other brands to penetrate, it can also represent a strong platform for renewed growth. In short it can literally breathe new life into aging products!

Like other market niches, the value pricing niche has very limited space. There is only enough room for one successful occupant—usually the tenant that gets there first. Value pricing is not a panacea for every senior citizen in the marketing ranks. But for brands that move quickly and boldly to claim the territory, the results can often far exceed expectations. Once again, the health and beauty aids category provides some of the best examples of successful value pricing niche marketing.

One of the first brands to recognize this opportunity was Suave shampoo back in the late 1970s. An old, well-known trademark, Suave was being battered by larger, richer competitors. A dramatic move was essential to reverse the brand's declining fortunes. Sensing an opening in the value pricing area, management significantly reduced price and initiated a concentrated burst of advertising to create consumer awareness of the price positioning.

The campaign exceeded even the most optimistic predictions. Within a few years Suave had become one of the largest unit-sellers in the shampoo category. Once established, the brand was able to maintain this position for many years with only minimal ad support. Furthermore the company was able to efficiently expand its business by introducing an extended line of hair-care products under the value pricing banner. In a category known for its faddishness and short product life cycles, Suave was able to successfully defy the odds over a prolonged period by pursuing a value pricing approach.

Another variation of the value pricing niche marketing strategy requires virtually no advertising expenditures. Under this superefficient scenario, a brand that is receiving competitive advertising support in one category expands into a related category, relying on the base brand's heritage and ongoing advertising to carry the new entry. For this rub-off to occur, consumers must perceive the base brand's benefits and the manufacturer's expertise to be meaningful and relevant in the new category.

Currently Arm & Hammer is attempting this tactic in the laundry products business. With their heavy-duty detergent and all-fabric bleach products, Arm & Hammer is striving to stake out the price/value positioning in these categories by riding on the coattails of its baking soda heritage and the widespread awareness of the Arm & Hammer name. Interestingly Church & Dwight, the owners of Arm & Hammer, arrived at this strategy through a lengthy process of trial and error.

According to an article in *The New York Times*, "The laundry detergent business turned out to be far more prosperous than the company had imagined when it introduced a phosphate-free detergent in 1970, but it took 15 years to come up with the right pricing strategy. Now detergents priced at a 20 percent discount to Procter & Gamble's Tide, the market leader, are Church & Dwight's biggest revenue generator."[7]

By linking the equity of an established brand to a new product in a different category, manufacturers can enhance the value component of the price/value equation. If utilized with judgment and discretion, this approach can be extremely effective in the marketplace. As such, this tactic should become increasingly popular with brand marketers in the years to come.

In a recent article on quality store brands, *American Demographics* predicted that the value pricing market will experience strong growth in the near future. This trend is expected to benefit both value brands and their store-brand counterparts. According to the article, "The [*Yankelovich*] *Monitor* study predicts that the social environment supporting store-brand growth will continue well into the 1990s. Store brands will flourish if the name, whether it is the retailer's or not, conveys information and reassurance to consumers. Otherwise the product runs the risk of being viewed as a generic, a category that consumers have decided is too risky for the money saved. . . . National brands are imitating store brands to exploit this market, and we can expect them to do so even more.[8]

NICHE POSSIBILITIES

With the cross-fertilization provided by globalization and market fragmentation, it seems that the possibilities for new niche products are almost endless, as is the potential of these brands to become major marketplace successes. To capitalize on these opportunities, corporations must begin to view the specialization of their products not as a liability, but as a valuable asset. If the architects of the Empire State Building had defined the scope of their building by the width of the lot, there would likely be a department store sitting on the Fifth Avenue site today. Instead of conventional thinking, they used an out-of-the-box approach to designing the space and created a building of vast, monumental proportions. Like these inspired designers, niche marketers today must dare to be innovative and look outside the box. If they do, they will discover that the potential to build a massive business often resides inconspicuously in a seemingly small base.

NOTES

1. Gerald A. Michaelson, "Niche Marketing in the Trenches," *Marketing Communications*, June 1988, p. 20.
2. Patricia Strand, "Is Any Niche Too Small for U.S. Automakers?" *Advertising Age*, April 9, 1990, p. 52.
3. "The Niche Word," *Forbes*, January 8, 1990, p. 307.
4. Ibid.
5. Thomas W. Osborne, "An American Mosaic," *Marketing Insights*, First issue, June 1989, p. 77.
6. Ibid., p. 78.
7. Barnaby J. Feder, "Baking Soda Maker Strikes Again," *The New York Times*, June 16, 1990, p. 8.
8. Chip Walker, "What's in a Name," *American Demographics*, February 1991, p. 54.

Chapter Ten

How to Market and Manage Niche Products

As discussed in the previous chapter, niche products can be almost infinite in their variety. As such, it is difficult to identify general marketing principles that have universal application for every conceivable product and circumstance. However, a few common denominators shared by successful niche brands can be extrapolated and applied to many new niche marketing opportunities. Managers who are mindful of these principles and who utilize them in niche marketing activities can greatly enhance the efficiency of their programs.

In addition to these marketing concepts, certain principles of management and internal organization can facilitate the development of niche brands and tend to increase the probability of their success. Just as a megabrand's extended product line requires a different kind of management organization—the strategic business unit (SBU)—so too does the specialized character of niche brands. These brands also call for a departure from the traditional brand-management system. However, unlike the SBU, the ideal structure for a niche marketing organization has yet to be precisely defined and widely implemented by major corporations.

In the discussion that follows, several unique aspects of marketing and managing successful niche products will be discussed. The goal of this discussion is to highlight key differences between niche marketing approaches and those techniques used to market and manage products with more general positionings.

PRODUCT NAME

Since specialization is the essence of niche marketing, a niche brand's name should communicate and reinforce the product's specialized point of difference. More than that, it should clearly lay claim to the particular market niche and preempt copy-cat competitors from invading this territory. Preemptive naming is most easily accomplished with niche products that base their specialization on their sharp product focus or their regional roots.

Preemptive naming played a major role in the success of some of America's earliest and best-known niche brands. For example, by naming their specialized detergent Woolite, American Home Products made it much more difficult for competitors to introduce other detergents for wool and fine washables. Likewise, Johnson & Johnson virtually owns a lucrative niche in the hair-care market due, in large part, to the simple, yet rock-solid name, Johnson's Baby Shampoo. Thanks largely to the proprietary character of the name Philadelphia Brand Cream Cheese, Kraft General Foods turned a specialty product into a huge, national business.

More recently, Conagra took title to the good nutrition niche in the frozen food category with its descriptive brand name, Healthy Choice. Thompson Medical accomplished a similar feat when it laid claim to the powdered drink niche in the diet aids market with the name Slim-Fast. And in the salad dressing business, the Kingsford division of Clorox took a popular western salad dressing—ranch—and turned it into a proprietary, national brand name: Hidden Valley Ranch salad dressing. What's in a name? In the business of niche marketing, it can be very much indeed.

PRICING

Throughout every corner of our society, specialization and higher prices seem to go hand in hand. This is certainly the case in consumer products marketing. Time and again consumers have shown themselves willing to pay more for a product that they believe does a particular, tough job better. Because of their specialization, most niche products are in a position to command premium prices versus their broadly based competitors. The obvious exceptions to this rule are niche products that pursue a value pricing strategy.

Generally consumers are less sensitive to the relative costs of niche products because many of these brands are used less frequently than mainstream products. Since the purchase cycle of niche brands is often more extended, consumers are less conscious of the costs of these products compared to products that they purchase on a weekly basis. This combination of a specialized benefit and an extended "use-up" rate often raises the price ceiling for niche products above that of general purpose brands.

Since premium pricing is, in most cases, one of the key sources of a niche brand's marketing leverage, every effort must be made to thoroughly understand a brand's pricing dynamics. Comprehensive research is required to determine the optimum price that will maximize both sales and profits. In particular, marketers must determine precisely how much consumers will pay for a niche product's specialized benefit before the price premium becomes so high that it stimulates large-scale defections, resulting in a net loss on the brand's bottom line.

After the optimum price point is identified, niche marketers must strenuously resist the temptation to cling to these earnings and amass excessive profits. To take full advantage of niche opportunities, managers must be willing to plow a large portion of their higher profits back into aggressive marketing programs. Otherwise, insufficient support may prematurely stunt business growth, making the reduced size of the brand niche a self-fulfilling prophecy.

As a result of premium pricing, niche products can afford to spend significantly more marketing money on a relative basis than larger, more competitively priced brands. This fact, coupled with the scarcity of direct competitors, can put niche products in an enviable marketing position. In the final analysis some niche products may not have the potential to grow into major brands.

However, most are capable of generating as much absolute profit as products two or three times their size. Even the smallest niche products can be large contributors to corporate profits.

MEDIA

Because of their specialized nature, many niche products may not require national mass media to support their introduction and early development. However, from the beginning there is still a pressing need for niche brands to communicate effectively with their consumers and retailers. In light of the special character of niche brands, both the form and the nature of their communications can vary dramatically from traditional advertising programs.

Targeted Media

Among product-focus niche brands, the overriding need is for media selectivity. Because of their sharp focus, these products must target their communications efforts at precisely defined consumer groups. In recent years this job has been made easier by the growth of new forms of targeted media. For example, the rapid growth of cable television has greatly improved marketers' ability to reach select target groups.

A headline in a special supplement of *Advertising Age* announced, "Program Selectivity Spurs Cable's Growth to Record Levels." According to the article, "Because of cable's dual revenue stream—advertising and subscriber fees—cable can afford to provide viewers with a wide range of specialized networks including all-news, popular music, weather, shopping, sports, ethnic programming, first-run movies, educational and cultural channels, and children's programming."[1] Due to cable's selectivity, many product-focus marketers have chosen to concentrate their advertising spending in this medium.

In addition to cable TV, there has been an explosion in the number of specialty print publications. The narrow editorial foci of these specialty publications allow niche marketers to selectively reach narrow target groups. Even traditional, mass magazines and newspapers are now offering split-runs that allow niche marketers to reach particular reader groups with the demographic and psychographic characteristics of their prime customer targets.

Regional Media

To say that regional niche products require regional media support is a comment on the obvious. However, putting together a regional media program that has impact requires much more than a computer-generated schedule of spot broadcast and local print. Media planners must acquire an understanding of regional markets from the inside out. They must be thoroughly familiar with the quirks and idiosyncrasies of the particular region of the country and its special breed of consumers.

A powerful regional media plan should include tactics such as tie-ins with local events, the use of local celebrities, and sponsorships of local shows and sports broadcasts. These kinds of regional programs are usually difficult to develop and execute from a distance. For this reason many large advertising agencies have set up regional spot-buying units in key areas across the country. Managers within these units are expected to develop a personal, first-hand knowledge of peculiarities of their respective markets. Then they are given the responsibility for buying, executing, and monitoring regional media programs to serve the agencies' national clients in these areas.

The phenomena of media regionalization was discussed recently in a well-known trade publication. According to the report,

> . . . national ad agencies like Bozell, Jacobs, Keynon & Eckhart, J. Walter Thompson, and Foote, Cone and Belding (FCB) have reorganized their buying departments on a regional basis. "We feel that there is enough complexity in each major market to justify the change," says the media director of one large New York agency. "Our buyers reside in their city and buy only for that city or region. . . ."[2]

But physical proximity is only part of the answer. Participation in important regional media programs and events usually entails a price premium. Therefore, to put together a high-impact regional program, advertisers must also be willing to make the mental leap from the objective world of cost-per-thousand to the subjective world of advertising judgment. As pressures for marketing efficiencies continue to grow within corporations, regional niche marketers must be staunch in their defense and use of more costly but effective programs. Otherwise the character of their regional plans will be severely compromised and the impact of the effort greatly diminished.

Nontraditional Media

Nontraditional media can be effective for all niche products, particularly distribution niche brands. Since many distribution niche products are not available in mass distribution outlets, traditional mass media do not represent an efficient communications approach. Instead, it is necessary to employ nontraditional media that more efficiently reach the limited group of customers who routinely shop in the brand's specialized distribution channel and avoid wasting messages on the many consumers who continue to shop in traditional outlets.

Point-of-sales communications can be especially effective in these types of situations. POS pieces can assume many forms, running the gamut from the familiar display on the drugstore counter or an ad on a supermarket shopping car, to a take-home patient brochure in a dentist's office or a five-minute hair-style video on a salon monitor. Despite the differences, all these vehicles share a common objective—to communicate a product's story at the point of purchase. The immediacy of these communications often make them even more effective than ads in the traditional media since there is little or no delay between commercial exposure and the consumer's purchase decision.

In addition to point-of-sale media, managers of all types of niche brands now recognize the importance of database marketing to the success of their efforts. Direct mail and other database techniques reach niche product users more selectively and efficiently than any mass media. Just as importantly, once the company has made contact with these users, database marketing can provide niche marketers with a method for continuing the dialogue and establishing a strong, ongoing relationship with these consumers.

RELATIONSHIP MARKETING

With customers sometimes few and far between, savvy niche marketers understand better than their large-brand counterparts the critical importance of building relationships with users once they have been identified. As expressed in a recent *Wall Street Journal* article, ". . . marketers believe that they can achieve greater cost effectiveness if they can establish a lasting dialogue or closer relationship with customers. The idea is that it is a lot easier to keep an existing customer than it is to start from scratch over and over again."[3]

One popular relationship marketing tactic used with increasing frequency by niche marketers is the newsletter. These letters combine product-selling messages with general-interest information broadly related to niche-brand usage to create an interesting package of material for consumers. For example, one successful brand of barbecue sauce publishes a regular newsletter on barbecuing, complete with expert tips and special recipes. To encourage continuous purchase, the letter also includes coupons and other premium offers.

Similarly the marketer of a niche drug product publishes a regular newsletter that provides users with the latest medical advice about their condition. The newsletter also includes a toll-free number to answer any health care questions and provides accounts of the successful experiences of other sufferers in dealing with their common health problem. Finally, it delivers high-value coupons to provide consumers with ongoing incentives for remaining in the franchise.

A regular newsletter can provide an extra benefit for niche distribution marketers. It offers them a means for improving their own relationships with the professional trade by giving the professional a method of strengthening his relationship with his consumers. For example, initial trial of distribution niche brands is often the result of personal, one-on-one recommendation by a pharmacist, a stylist, or some other professional.

Once the initial purchase has taken place, newsletters and subsequent consumer communications can be personalized by the manufacturer so that messages and purchase incentives come directly from the professional to the customer. Not only can this personalization strengthen the link between the professional and the consumer, but it can also enhance the professional's stature in the customer's eyes since he or she is seen as the source of valuable information and offers. At the same time, the manufacturer's relationships with both the consumer and the professional are solidified.

Because distribution niche marketing often involves the professional in the selling process, most successful companies supplement their personal contacts with their professional target audience with ads in professional journals and ongoing direct marketing campaigns. For these marketers developing relationships with these professionals is as critical as with consumers. In the end, perceptive niche distribution marketers recognize the two groups as interrelated and equally important to their long-term success.

PUBLIC RELATIONS

Finally a nontraditional medium that can be used very effectively by all niche marketers is public relations. By virtue of their specialization, niche products often have a built-in "news value." This news value can be enhanced by a public relations professional, who can direct the story to editors and producers in the print and electronic media whose regular audiences are most likely to be interested in the new product.

For example, a publicist for a new allergy medicine would typically send press releases and other information about the new product to the health editors at magazines, newspapers, and television and radio stations. In an age when the media are looking for material to fill air time and page space, this type of product news often generates good coverage at a very low cost to the manufacturer. For many niche marketers public relations can be the most efficient communications vehicle of all.

ADVERTISING

In situations where niche products do advertise through traditional media, it is important that their communications be single-minded in approach. Clear communication of the brand's specialization is essential to success. In the initial phases managers must be careful not to expand the expression of the product's selling message in an attempt to broaden its appeal. To the degree that a niche brand's advertising can *precisely communicate* the product's unique rational and emotional benefits, and thereby claim this territory as its own, it makes it much more difficult for subsequent entries to challenge its position.

Price/Value Advertising

In view of the broad appeal of value-priced niche products, advertising for these products is usually placed in the mass media. However, while the media selection may be typical of most brands, the message strategies and spending levels for value-priced brands are not. As previously discussed, the economics of value-priced brands translate into advertising support levels far below higher priced products. In some cases value-priced products do not advertise at all.

When value-priced brands do advertise, their advertising tends to occur in short concentrated bursts. Since these bursts are often timed to take place in conjunction with major promotional events, much price/value advertising tends to be promotional in nature. In addition to the standard value pricing message, these commercials also flag some added promotional savings.

Many value pricing niche marketers invest a disproportionate amount of their marketing dollars in FSIs (freestanding inserts) in Sunday newspapers. While hardly a hospitable medium for most advertising messages, the FSI "discount" environment can actually reinforce the value pricing story. The value message is telegraphically communicated through the equity of the brand name. When the everyday low price is sweetened by a special promotional offer, the medium and the message can come together to create an extremely persuasive package.

PROMOTION

In the area of promotion, niche marketers benefit from the fundamental fact that they do not have to please all of the people all of the time. Because of their specialized character, they can custom-tailor both trade and consumer promotions to best meet the needs of their customers. When properly executed, this customization provides important advantages over mass-marketed products.

Consider the mass marketer of a nonprescription cold remedy who must design the major annual cold and flu promotion to appeal to buyers and customers in food, drug, mass merchandiser, and warehouse outlets. Now consider a niche distribution marketer of a similar product who is focused only on the drugstore business. Surely the niche marketer is in a better position to create a program with high impact on the actual drug buyers: the pharmacists and the drugstore consumers. Now compare the niche wood-cleaning product that can build a high-interest consumer event around this benefit to the general cleaning brand that must often rely on borrowed-interest techniques for broad appeal. Again the niche product's narrow focus offers clear advantages in designing an effective promotion program.

Sampling

In building a niche product, or any brand, sampling is a key consumer promotion activity. In many cases targeted sampling programs are already available that can help niche marketers efficiently reach their target consumers. For example, Procter & Gamble utilized a number of preexisting sampling and couponing programs for Dreft baby detergent in order to reach the niche brand's primary target—first-time mothers.

According to a spokesperson from Saatchi & Saatchi, Dreft's advertising agency,

> Dreft fielded a hospital sampling program in key markets and distributed coupons via a highly targeted promotion and direct mail packages designed to reach prenatal mothers, new mothers, and new Hispanic mothers.
>
> Additionally, our media selection followed the same stringent targeting—we placed our advertising in publications and television programming that were able to reach a high concentration of the core target with a minimum of waste.[4]

As a result of this targeted promotion and advertising program, Saatchi & Saatchi reported that Dreft's sales increased 10 percent during 1990 in an otherwise stagnant market.

Professional Endorsements

Another promotional technique that is particularly effective for niche marketers is endorsement by professional associations, trade groups, and leading companies in related fields. For example, there is no question that the endorsement of the American Dental Association played a major role in the success of the Interplak electric toothbrush. Likewise, Dreft used the endorsement of a respected baby clothes manufacturer, Carter's, to add credibility to its baby detergent positioning.

STRUCTURAL BARRIERS TO NICHE MARKETING SUCCESS

In addition to the promotional tactics described above, regional niche marketers can realize other built-in promotional advantages simply as a result of their "up close and personal" understanding of local customers and competitors. Although many mass marketers have recognized the benefits of a regional orientation and are shifting their promotional emphasis from national to regional events, some may never be able to catch up. The fundamental structure of their marketing and sales organizations is working against them.

As one industry observer explains,

> Most of the past several decades have been devoted to building national brands with national advertising and promotion. So a reversal—concentrating on regional products, advertising and/or promotion—isn't expected to be quick or easy. "Fast food and beverage companies have always done it . . . but their channels of distribution are different, they have field forces," says Walter Coddington, president of Coddington Chadwick Meyerson NY. "The question for package goods companies now is how to execute it. The brand management system isn't set up for it. In McDonald's world, they would handle the situation through multiple local agencies who also do promotion. A package goods company has a few ad agencies and several sales promotion agencies."[5]

The structural disadvantages this consultant is describing not only affect the implementation of regional promotions, they can negatively affect every aspect of a mass marketer's niche-brand program, from product development through plan execution. In short,

The structure of a traditional marketing organization can severely inhibit that organization's ability to compete successfully in the niche marketing arena.

As niche products continue to play an increasingly important role in the battle against the megabrands, many corporations will be compelled to carefully examine and redesign internal organizational structures to build support for niche-brand marketing activities. This reassessment will require fundamental changes in basic assumptions about the market and in business practices. It will call for exceptional amounts of flexibility and out-of-the-box thinking.

THE ACQUISITION STRATEGY

It is no coincidence that the majority of successful niche brands within major corporations today are there as the result of acquisitions. Throughout U.S. industry the pattern is now well established. Over a period of years, an entrepreneurial operation creates and builds a niche business and then sells out to a large company with the resources to expand the product on a much larger scale. Most of the time, the founders walk away from the transaction with their pockets full of money.

Until now corporations have relied mainly on acquisition to produce niche brands because they have not been able to regularly innovate and develop these products in-house. But acquisition is a strategy replete with inherent difficulties. To begin with, acquisitions are unpredictable. There is no guarantee that appropriate new products will be available when corporations need them to meet long-range growth objectives. Then there is the matter of cost. Since entrepreneurs place a high price tag on their own inventiveness, acquisitions can be much more costly than internal product development. Generally, in the bidding for a successful niche product, it is a seller's market and interested corporations must pay the going rate.

REINVENTING THE CORPORATION

To compete successfully and consistently in the niche marketplace, corporations must essentially internalize the structure, processes, and techniques of small niche companies. Within their own niche development groups, they must be willing to dramatically alter the corporate culture to encourage greater risk-taking, reward innovation, and support nontraditional business management practices. They must recognize that niche marketers operate according to a different business model and therefore "march to the beat of a different drummer." For many large organizations, this is not an easy task.

Venture Groups

Thus far, the closest that many corporations have come to creating this environment is venture groups. Under this system, new-product projects that represent dramatic departures from the company's basic business are spun off into separate venture groups. Within these freestanding organizations, members of all key disciplines—R&D, marketing, sales, etc.—come together as a team to create a start-up operation. The common charter of venture groups is to foster entrepreneurship with the backing of a financially strong company.

While the concept seems solid, most venture groups have experienced very limited success. For every corporation that has established such a group, another has shut one down. While early intentions seem honorable, venture participants and their corporate sponsors are often unable to abandon the old ways of thinking. They bring much historical baggage with them into the new enterprise. This baggage often weighs down their problem-solving capabilities and ultimately causes them to fail.

In considering the poor success rate of corporate venture groups in building niche products, there appear to be three major barriers that these operations often fail to overcome:

1. The immediate size of the opportunity.
2. The need for a new organization structure and tactics.
3. The extended time lines of niche projects.

Any or all of these issues can cause venture management to prematurely abandon promising niche products that, if properly nourished, could have become significant businesses.

Assessing the Size of Niche Opportunities

Over the years most corporations have set minimum sales goals as part of their new-product evaluation criteria. These goals reflect the company's collective experience regarding how much volume is required to build and sustain a profitable business. If preliminary estimates of ongoing volume (usually three years out) fall below this predetermined point, the project is canceled. When it comes to evaluating niche-brand potential, these criteria are inappropriate because they are based on the company's experience selling mass-marketed products in the traditional manner.

Comparing niche brands to broadly based products is tantamount to comparing kangaroos to elephants. Niche brands often have significantly different pricing and profit structures, distribution systems, and geographic trading areas. To apply the same evaluation yardstick to these products is inappropriate and misleading. Yet while companies may pay lip service to this reality, many continue to view niche opportunities through the old, familiar lens. As a result, while waiting for the $25 million mass-market opportunity that never comes, they pass over several profitable, $8–10 million niche opportunities that were there for the taking.

Redesigning the Structure

To be successful in the niche arena, organizations must reinvent themselves and embrace management structures that are dramatically different from the norm. For example, in entrepreneurial organizations, work groups are often leaner and less hierarchical. Within such a setting the marketing manager may no longer play the leadership role but participate as an equal partner along with other team members. Many old-line managers are simply incapable of making this transition. Try as they might to adjust, it just never feels right.

Even when managers can accept the new internal structure, they must still master a whole set of nontraditional marketing skills. For example, some might have to learn to interact with a new class of trade, become familiar with the idiosyncrasies of a regional market, or utilize direct marketing in place of mass media programs. In their enthusiasm to move ahead (and under corporate pressure to shorten the developmental time frame), some will not allow themselves adequate time to absorb and master new management approaches and techniques. Denying their own ignorance and inexperience, they may rush programs to market with insufficient understanding and quickly fail.

Extending Time Lines

When entering unfamiliar niche territory, it is critically important that venture managers proceed slowly and with caution. Ultimately it is this different pace that poses the biggest obstacle for corporations seeking to succeed in niche marketing. Unlike other brands, the "biological clock" of most niche products ticks at a much slower rate. These products take longer to gestate, longer to develop, and longer to reach maturity. Marketers must adjust their own sense of timing to match the realities of these markets. For marketers accustomed to instant gratification and immediate results, the extended development time line of niche products can seem agonizingly long.

In short, to successfully manage the niche marketing process, corporations must overcome a myriad of intellectual and psychological stumbling blocks that have caused the demise of many internally generated niche projects. On the financial side they must accept the fact that today's consumer markets are highly fragmented and that niche product sales volume projections may not always meet the mass-market criteria of the past. They must look beyond a brand's sales during its early years and recognize the potential for substantial, long-term growth.

On the organizational side, many corporations have already taken the critical first step by establishing separate venture groups. Now they must step up to the fact that the tensions and confusions created by nontraditional organizational structures and practices are not going to solve themselves. They must be willing to address these issues directly and proactively with concrete policies and programs.

NEW SKILLS AND NEW MIND-SETS

Within these new organizations, employee and management training must be assigned the highest priority. Training programs must not only concentrate on the skills required for niche marketing success but also on the supervisory skills required to manage and motivate new venture teams. Management skills that focus on employee participation and empowerment must be finely honed if these new projects are to prosper.

Finally, when it comes to product development time lines, management must develop a new mind-set. Undoubtedly the development period for niche brands is more extended than for mass products. When building niche products, managers cannot afford to think quarter-to-quarter or even year-to-year. They must be prepared to invest and commit to longer blocks of time. While the payout period will be more extended, when it finally comes it will be substantial. What's more, the corporation will be the developer and owner of a valuable brand equity with remarkable consumer staying power.

To succeed with niche brands, management must acknowledge that these brands may not fit within the traditional corporate environment. Instead, it may make more business sense to maintain them as permanent, stand-alone units within the company. While this may not be the most efficient organization structure on paper, in reality an autonomous operation left on its own to do what it does best will often achieve maximum productivity.

For most major corporations niche marketing holds out exciting prospects for substantial growth. However, these prospects can never be fully realized when approached with a business-as-usual mentality. Successful niche marketing demands a nontraditional outlook that, in turn, spawns fundamental changes in traditional organizational structures and management practices.

As we have already seen, many companies are resisting these changes. Yet despite their resistance, such changes are necessary for long-term, competitive success. In the future, corporations that move aggressively to seize these new opportunities and rise to meet the challenge of change will be richly rewarded. Those that do not are likely to be left behind—stalled in the stagnant backwaters of the marketing past.

NOTES

1. Cable Television Advertising Bureau, "Cable TV Facts," *Advertising Age*, February 11, 1991.
2. Brad Edmondson, "Targeting America's Hot Spots," *American Demographics*, January 1988, p. 29.
3. Richard Gibson, "Marketers' Mantra: Reap More with Less," *The Wall Street Journal*, March 22, 1991, p. B1.
4. "1990 Winners," *The Effie Gold Awards: Case Studies in Advertising Effectiveness*, The American Marketing Association/The American Association of Advertising Agencies, 1991, p. 44.
5. *Advertising Business Report*, July 1987, p. 5.

Chapter Eleven

Niche Marketing Case Histories

To prosper as a niche marketer, it is essential that a company begin by freeing itself from the bonds of traditional thinking and business practices. Because of the huge differences in size and tangible resources, it is impossible for smaller products to beat the megabrands at their own game. Success requires a different perspective, a high degree of marketing innovation, and an entrepreneurial flair.

These qualities characterize each of the niche marketing success stories reviewed in this chapter. In the world of niche marketing there is no place for a business-as-usual mentality. Niche marketing is one of the most fluid and dynamic areas of contemporary marketing. As a result it has attracted many of the industry's most creative thinkers and spawned many of the most exciting product hits.

The case studies that follow illustrate the four distinct approaches to niche market product development described in Chapter 9. Collectively these product histories provide a representative sample of the range of niche marketing activities taking place throughout the United States. In addition, some niche marketing flops will also be discussed, and the key problems that these products experienced will be identified.

NICHE MARKETING HITS

FOCUSED PRODUCT POSITIONING

Case Study 1: Healthy Choice

Remarkably, one of the biggest new-product successes of 1989 was a niche product. Inspired by the heart attack of its chairman, Conagra Inc., the Omaha-based food company, introduced Healthy Choice, a low-calorie, low-cholesterol, low-sodium frozen food line. Before the year was out, Healthy Choice rang up $150 million in sales and had the big players in the frozen food business frantically regrouping.

Because of limited freezer space, frozen foods are believed by many industry experts to be the most competitive supermarket category. With well-established competitors like Lean Cuisine (Stouffer's), Le Menu (Campbell's), and Weight Watchers, there appeared to be little opportunity for a new, health-oriented brand. But by means of a narrow, focused positioning, Healthy Choice was able to claim a prominent position in the freezer case and rapidly build a significant market share.

In launching Healthy Choice, Conagra broke two of the conventional category rules. First, it introduced the product into the stagnant, male-oriented frozen dinner segment of the market, not the fast-growing, female-oriented frozen entree segment. Second, it positioned the brand as a "health" product. Previously this term had been used to describe poor-tasting, low-calorie entries.

Conagra was able to make this niche positioning work because it linked the brand's health promise primarily to the product's low-cholesterol benefit—an issue of great concern to Americans today, especially men. In addition, through effective advertising the company was also able to portray Healthy Choice not as a product for "sick" people but, instead, for all health-conscious consumers. Finally Conagra also developed a product line that delivered improved taste, a benefit that appealed to mainstream Americans.

This finely focused positioning was so persuasive it actually drew substantial numbers of males into the frozen food category for the first time. According to a recent analysis in *Marketing and Media Decisions*, "Somewhat surprisingly, this bland-sounding product has taken the supermarket frozen food section by storm. Within months of its January 1989 introduction, the green-boxed 14-item line grabbed a 25 percent share in the $700 million frozen dinner market. . . . Healthy Choice now is the number-one premium frozen dinner and has expanded the category rather than just cannibalize sales."[1]

Caught off guard, Stouffer's and Campbell's have been scrambling to catch up. Stouffer's has introduced a comparable health line called Right Course, while Campbell's has repositioned the Le Menu Light Style line to stress its nutritional value. But while these category leaders have been covering their flanks, Conagra has been moving ahead aggressively into their territory. In 1990 the company began rolling out 10 new entrees into the mostly female $1.7 billion frozen entree market.

In addition Conagra has begun using nontraditional channels of distribution. According to a recent article, "January [1990] saw the quiet introduction of Professional Choice, a 10-item line targeted to the needs of doctors, hospitals, and 'behavior modification centers' such as weight loss clinics."[2]

Healthy Choice has clearly demonstrated that a niche product does not have to be relegated to the ranks of a small business. On the strength of a focused product positioning, the brand has become a major category player in an incredibly brief period of time.

Case Study 2: Tilex

In the mid-70s Clorox spotted a niche opportunity in the crowded home cleaning category. Although already packed with numerous brands in a variety of product forms, such as disinfectants, dilutable cleaners, and sprays, there was still one cleaning job where available products fell short—removing mildew stains from bathroom surfaces. As it turned out, Clorox was in an excellent position to satisfy this unmet need.

The company knew that nothing was more effective at getting rid of this difficult problem than its own mainstay ingredient, Clorox liquid bleach. In fact many of its own consumers were already using Clorox bleach for this purpose. Therefore Clorox concluded that if it could develop a specialty, bleach-based product focused exclusively on mildew removal, it could claim ownership of a whole new product area.

The first step was to develop the product itself. The company began by reviewing the product formulation and adjusting the level of bleach to make it most effective at removing mildew. Next, product packaging was considered. Common sense told the marketing team that it needed a more convenient method of application than a standard bottle. The obvious choice was a spray container that allowed consumers to apply the ingredients directly to the mildew.

That was the easy part! Then came the more difficult challenge of positioning and marketing the product to preempt competitors and permanently own this new area for the Clorox Company. To accomplish this task, both the product name and a succinct description of the new product class were key. In both respects Clorox's decisions were on target.

With the brand name Tilex, the company chose a name that immediately and telegraphically communicated the essential fact that this was a specialty product for cleaning tile. Then it added the descriptor, "Instant mildew stain remover." The descriptor provided two additional pieces of important information:

1. This was a product for removing mildew.
2. The product went to work instantly upon contact.

The final assignment was to reinforce this focused positioning and communicate it to the consumer through advertising. To highlight the benefits of Tilex, Clorox chose a commercial approach that contrasted the old method of removing mildew stains—a brush and cleanser—with the convenient, new Tilex approach. At the core of the commercials was a product demonstration in which time-lapse photography showed Tilex quickly eliminating mildew stains with no scrubbing. The commercial theme line was a straightforward statement of what the viewer had just witnessed, "Tilex removes mildew stains in minutes with no scrubbing."

Introduced in 1979 at a premium price, Tilex caught on quickly among its specialty target. The relatively small size of the

Tilex business precluded massive levels of first-year marketing support. However, over the next 10 years Clorox continued to spend aggressively behind the brand to maximize awareness and trial. The brand's high level of spending relative to category size served to keep would-be competitors from entering this niche. Today Tilex still commands a leading and highly profitable share of the instant mildew stain remover segment it created 15 years ago.

REGIONAL MARKETING

Case Study 3: Celestial Seasonings

In 1969 an unlikely entrepreneur named Mo Siegel cofounded Celestial Seasonings, a small herbal tea company in Boulder, Colorado. What transpired over the next 20 years provides a classic example of successful regional niche marketing. It also provides some important lessons about the difficulties of absorbing an entrepreneurial company into a large and highly structured organization.

As many people know, herbal teas are not really teas at all but blends of flowers, leaves, roots, and the stems of edible plants. These blends are steeped in water, yielding a natural, caffeine-free beverage. According to local folklore, Mo Siegel brewed the first Celestial Seasonings teas with herbs he picked himself in the Rocky Mountains.

The Celestial Seasonings concept fit perfectly with an emerging consumer attitude that was partly a remnant of the 60s counterculture and partly a preview of the health consciousness of the 70s. Within a few years the company was brewing a broad line of teas with such whimsical names as Red Zinger, Sleepytime, Mandarin Orange Spice, and Wild Forest Blackberry. With a prospering regional business, the company began to expand its niche brand nationally.

The roll-out efforts met with only partial success. While Celestial Seasonings managed to gain distribution in much of the country, it did not have the corporate clout required to totally penetrate large chains nor the marketing spending power to aggressively promote and advertise the brand. Then in 1984 the company was sold to the giant food marketer, Kraft General Foods.

At first the Celestial Seasonings/Kraft combination seemed a marriage made in heaven. According to a *Business Week* report, "Kraft helped increase Celestial's supermarket shelf space and boosted its ad budget 10-fold, to $6 million. Sales increased 50 percent in four years . . . to $40 million a year."[3] Driven by Celestial Seasonings, herb teas had become a $90 million niche of the $1.2 billion tea category.

Unfortunately, the happy union was short-lived. Conflicts soon began to develop between Kraft management and the Celestial Seasonings group over advertising strategy and product development. Even more disturbing were the clashes between the two corporate cultures and differences in management style. The two groups just couldn't seem to come together.[4]

Eventually the stresses that built up between the two organizations, coupled with a strategic decision by Kraft to wind down its beverage business, brought about a parting of the ways. In 1988 Kraft sold Celestial Seasonings back to its management in a leveraged buyout. The company had returned to its entrepreneurial roots.

Today Celestial Seasonings is looking to expand its herbal tea niche into the related gourmet and decaffeinated tea categories. The company is also planning expansion into the food service business and the growing international market. Drawing upon the strengths of its regional roots and distinct corporate culture, the Celestial Seasonings business appears to be again in a growth mode.

Case Study 4: Murphy's Oil Soap

For 86 years it was marketed exclusively in a single region of the country. Eventually it became the number-one product in its class in that part of the world. Based on its local strength, it began a region-by-region roll-out in 1976. Fourteen years later the brand achieved national distribution and attained the number-six position in a major product category.

The brand is Murphy's Oil Soap and the product's 100-year journey from a small town in Ohio to a significant contender in the all-purpose cleaning category provides a fascinating example of successful regional niche marketing. A family-run business, Murphy's became the number-one all-purpose cleaner in the Great Lakes region by touting its wood-cleaning abilities. In 1976 research confirmed that this positioning could have national appeal since neither ammonia-based cleaners like Mr. Clean nor abrasives like Comet could be used on wooden surfaces.

According to a recent article, "Paul Murphy, son of patriarch M. J. Murphy, says it took until 1976 to break out of regional distribution because the sales force didn't want to drive more than one day from company headquarters in Beachwood, Ohio. The family used food brokers for its first foray east."[4]

The roll-out process was slow and deliberate since the company was funding this effort itself. Syracuse was the first expansion market, followed by the New England region. Murphy's chose spot television as the introductory medium. The high costs of sales promotion were particularly onerous for the small company.

In a recent interview Paul Murphy observed, "Frankly, if we were starting out today with what we started with in 1976, I don't think we could, or would do it. . . . It cost us a lot of money over the past few years to get the product national, and lot of promotional allowances and fees."[5]

In spite of the costs, the expansion has paid out handsomely. According to industry sources, "The company's total sales jumped 50 percent in 1980, and 40 percent in 1982. Today [1990] Murphy's Oil Soap retail sales are between $30 million and $35 million, eight times larger than in 1980."[6]

Clearly Murphy's strong performance in the national market is directly linked to its wood-cleaning positioning. But to attribute the brand's success solely to this positioning would be an oversimplification. Murphy's brand image and consumer popularity are strongly rooted in the product's midwestern, regional heritage.

For example, the name Murphy's Oil Soap strongly evokes middle America and traditional midwestern values. The brand's "Great Houses" advertising campaign—running since 1986—features grand old houses that dramatize the beauty of wood and the special qualities of a wood-cleaning product. To this day the business continues to have a regional skew toward the midwest and east—areas with older cities and a greater number of old, wooden houses.

Recently the brand began to expand its positioning beyond pure wood cleaning. Package copy for Murphy's spray formula, the line's most recent entry, proclaims, "Cleans wood surfaces . . . and more! Kitchen appliances, countertops, painted walls, washable wallpaper, fiberglass tubs, tile, car interiors, leather, vinyl, and more." But even with a broader positioning, Murphy's basic appeal continue to be a tied to its regional roots with the package copy reminding consumers that Murphy's has been "cleaning American homes for over 75 years." In July 1991, the Colgate-Palmolive Company formally acknowledged the strength of Murphy's niche positioning and the loyalty of its user franchise by acquiring the brand for an undisclosed sum.

EXCLUSIVE CHANNELS OF DISTRIBUTION

Case Study 5: Interplak

In the early 80s a group of entrepreneurs in Ft. Collins, Colorado, founded a company called Interplak. Their sole product was a patented electric toothbrush with individual revolving bristles. What transpired over the next five years was a textbook case of successful niche marketing through an exclusive channel of distribution.

There was nothing orthodox about the distribution outlet that was selected. It was not mass merchandisers, drugstores, or even a catalog. Instead Interplak selected dentists as its exclusive channel of distribution. By means of a direct sales force, Interplak promoted the oral hygiene benefits of its patented toothbrush directly to dental professionals. In turn, those dentists who were convinced of the product's benefits sold it directly to their patients—right out of their offices.

Interplak referred to its toothbrush as a plaque removal system and supported this claim with evidence from clinical studies that supported its plaque-removing capabilities. Dentists were persuaded by what Interplak had to say, and product sales gave their practice some additional income. Soon many were promoting the product.

Not surprisingly these professional recommendations carried a lot of weight with consumers. Despite its $100 price tag—more than twice the cost of competitive electric toothbrushes—Interplak sales grew briskly. According to one user survey, "63 percent of Interplak users were recommended to the product by their dentists, and 90 percent of the users said Interplak met or exceeded expectations."[7]

To add to the credibility of these professional recommendations, Interplak applied for and received the endorsement of the American Dental Association for its product as an effective tool against gum disease. About the same time, the company extended its distribution system by offering the product as an exclusive item in the Sharper Image catalog. Stimulated by these developments, sales continued to climb.

Enter contact lens giant Bausch & Lomb. Looking to expand its health care franchise into the oral-care market, Bausch & Lomb acquired Interplak in 1988. Bausch & Lomb expanded distribution into department stores and pharmacies and initiated the product's first TV advertising campaign. At the same time the company continued to actively promote the product to dental professionals. For 1989 Interplak sales were in the neighborhood of $100 million.[8]

In 1990 Bausch & Lomb continued its expansion program. First the company moved into mass merchandisers and began to promote replacement bristles and a toothpaste made especially for the Interplak device. To strengthen the brand's position with dentists, the company introduced Interprob, a device that helps dentists chart periodontal disease.

In the span of just a few years, astute marketers had taken a niche distribution product and built it into a huge consumer franchise. The strength of Interplak today, as in the past, is the brand's special relationship with the dental professional. This relationship, coupled with the endorsement of the American Dental Association, still separates Interplak from the pack and gives it an elevated position in the world of oral health care marketing.

Case Study 6: Metamucil

The kind of niche distribution success that Interplak accomplished in three years, Metamucil accomplished over a much longer period of time. Both brands built their business through an exclusive channel of distribution before rolling out into the broader market.

In the case of Metamucil, the distribution outlet was drugstores. By selling the brand exclusively through drugstores and promoting it exclusively to physicians, G. D. Searle built Metamucil into America's number-one laxative brand. The ongoing support and recommendations of doctors and pharmacists were the foundations of Metamucil's success.

In the early 80s Searle decided to build on this success by expanding distribution into food stores and initiating consumer advertising. Unlike most laxatives Metamucil is not chemically based. It is a fiber-based product that is mixed with water. As a result it works more gently on the system. The product's unique ingredient and mode of action had traditionally been one of the primary factors behind its strong professional support. It also became the focus of its consumer advertising campaign.

While Metamucil sales did respond to this new program, Searle was not a consumer marketing company and did not have the consumer marketing expertise to maximize the brand's volume potential. This problem was instantly alleviated when Procter & Gamble acquired the company in 1985. P&G had placed a high priority on developing its consumer health care business. Immediately it began to invest substantial resources in developing its new brand.

Under P&G's stewardship, food store distribution improved immediately as did the quality of Metamucil's consumer advertising and promotional programs. P&G also embarked on a drive to improve product taste and texture, Metamucil's only major consumer negative. Today, as a result of these activities, Metamucil has tightened its grip on the leadership position in the $700 million laxative market.

In addition, it is now clear that P&G's aspirations for Metamucil extend far beyond the laxative category. Clinical studies have shown that Metamucil's fiber ingredient (psyllium) can help reduce serum cholesterol levels that can cause heart disease. The company currently has a petition before the FDA to make cholesterol reduction claims on its packaging and in consumer advertising.

As discussed in a recent *Advertising Age* story, "Obviously longer term, Procter is hoping to make health claims for Metamucil," said Jay Freedman, an analyst at Kidder, Peabody & Co. "They'll be trying to get an incremental kick by getting people to view Metamucil not just as a laxative but almost as a health product."[9]

To lay the groundwork for this new positioning, P&G has introduced a new fiber-wafer line extension and is supporting the launch with a national TV and print campaign that positions the wafer as "fiber therapy for busy people." In addition, P&G has also begun to actively promote Metamucil in 19 countries around the world.

From a successful niche laxative sold only in drugstores, P&G is now transforming Metamucil into a global brand with a potentially vast target market. Yet it is important to remember that, even today, this imposing international structure rests on the solid foundation of the brand's professional niche heritage.

VALUE PRICING

Case Study 7: Barbasol

As the costs of advertising and promotion continue to escalate, some of America's most established brands are finding themselves priced out of the market, unable to compete dollar for dollar with their megabrand competitors. In this situation, reducing the level of the brand's marketing spending and shifting to a value pricing strategy can be a highly effective niche marketing strategy.

What makes the strategy viable is the preexisting awareness and quality image that well-established brands enjoy with consumers. These products do not have to convince consumers of their value; they simply have to make them aware of the new, low price. In 1984 the Leeming/Pacquin division of Pfizer created just such a value pricing niche-marketing program for one of its most venerable brand names—Barbasol shaving cream.

Years before, the company had suspended advertising for the product because of the tight economics of competing in the shaving cream category. Management had decided to reduce Barbasol's price 20 to 30 percent below Colgate, the other leading brand, and to market the product on a value pricing platform. Because of the brand's quality image among older consumers, the value pricing positioning had worked well for a number of years. However, as the brand's core users aged, there was a need to increase awareness of Barbasol's value pricing story among younger consumers.

To accomplish this objective, Pfizer planned a limited, one-time advertising campaign designed to raise awareness of the value pricing story and generate new trial. The company reasoned that if it could stimulate consumers to purchase Barbasol once, it was likely that they would become regular users. More pragmatically, in light of the brand's low price structure, a limited campaign was literally all the company could afford.

To communicate the value pricing story, Pfizer chose a humorous commercial depicting a wealthy man who, despite the fact that he could afford any brand, chose Barbasol because it gave him a "great shave at a great price." Although the advertising ran nationally for only six months, it was extremely effective. The effort pushed Barbasol well beyond the competition and firmly established the brand as the number-one unit seller.

Pfizer did not stop there. Sensing an opportunity to extend the Barbasol name and the value pricing story into related categories, the company introduced Barbasol stick antiperspirant about a year later. The primary target for the stick was men who were users of Barbasol shaving cream. Like the shaving cream, Barbasol stick was priced significantly lower than its major competitors.

To create awareness of this new line item, Pfizer utilized the same humorous commercial format. This time the rich man was using Barbasol stick. To date, Barbasol stick has succeeded in carving out a value pricing niche in the antiperspirant market. While not on the scale of Barbasol shaving cream, the stick has been a successful venture and has expanded Barbasol's position in the health and beauty aid category.

Most recently Pfizer has launched a Barbasol shaving gel in an attempt to take on Edge and further increase the brand's shaving business. In light of the proven strength of the Barbasol name and the appeal of the value pricing niche, there is every reason to expect that this product will also be a success.

Case Study 8: ScotTowels

Until the late 50s ScotTowels had the paper towel business basically to itself. Then in 1957 Procter & Gamble introduced its first entry—Bounty—after acquiring the Charmin Paper Company. Since then, competition in the paper towel category has never been the same.

P&G backed the Bounty launch with heavy marketing spending and an advertising campaign that featured the brand's unique two-ply composition and its "quicker picker upper" absorbency claim. Unaccustomed to tough competition, the Scott Paper Company struggled to mount an effective response.

Ultimately Scott elected to develop two new brands—Viva and Job Squad—to answer Procter's challenge on the performance front. However, the problem with the flagship brand was more difficult. After years of changing strategies and share declines, the brand finally settled on a value pricing positioning. While Bounty was a technically superior product, ScotTowels did provide excellent quality at an excellent price. Advertising began to feature Scott's "sheets per roll" advantage, and the business stabilized.

For 15 years ScotTowels never wavered. In 1988 the brand was still pursuing a value pricing approach. However, the cast of characters in the paper towel category had changed dramatically. Generics now controlled a market share comparable to Scot-Towels, and these products were challenging the brand's market position. At the other end of the spectrum, Bounty, now the market leader with over a 20 percent share, was continuing to advertise and promote heavily. Scott management concluded that a change in strategic direction was in order.

Having laid the groundwork for many years, ScotTowels decided to pursue a pure value pricing niche-marketing strategy. Knowing the Scott brand name was synonymous with quality paper products, corporate management elected to suspend all consumer advertising. As described by *Adweek*,

> Advertisers have entertained the notion before but few have acted on it as decisively as Scott Paper. In 1985, the Philadelphia-based company was a major advertiser, spending $30 million a year to advertise its brands. Last year it spent only about $6 million.
>
> At that level it didn't need the services of J. Walter Thompson

USA, whose relationship with Scott goes back 61 years, or BBDO Worldwide, which has been with Scott for 20 years. Instead, Scott will look for a smaller agency with direct marketing and promotional expertise.[10]

In addition to stepped-up promotional activities, Scott even incorporated its value pricing approach into its product development efforts. In late 1990 the company began testing a new Scot-Towels line extension called Mega Roll. According to a recent report, "Scott's Mega Roll pitch is that it contains double the number of towels of the other leading brand (Bounty) for much less than double the price at retail."[11]

Mega Roll is the most recent stage in the evolution of Scot-Towels' value pricing strategy. With consumer equity built up over 61 years, it is difficult to imagine how any competitor could dislodge the brand from its current market niche.

NICHE MARKETING FLOPS

The key causes of niche product failures are essentially the same factors that can derail any new product. However, in niche product marketing there often appears to be even less tolerance for error. Because extreme specialization is the hallmark of a niche brand, extreme precision is the basic requirement in the development of such products and in the execution of their marketing programs.

Once established, the high degree of specialization that defines niche brands provides greater insulation from competitive threat than do the more generalized positionings and programs of broadly based products. This principle holds true regardless of the type of niche product or its marketing approach. What's more, through smart, aggressive marketing, niche products can maintain this competitive insulation for many years.

In examining the causes of niche product failures, three primary factors are at work. These factors include:

1. Lack of a meaningful product difference.
2. No significant consumer need or demand.
3. Poor product performance or quality.

NO PRODUCT DIFFERENCE

Because of the specialized nature of niche product marketing, there is rarely room for numerous competitors. In order to break into an existing market niche, a product must offer a significant performance advantage over the dominant niche brand. Over the years there have been numerous examples of aspiring niche products that failed because they lacked this key point of differentiation.

One of the most notable examples took place in the late 70s when Bristol-Myers challenged Woolite's control of the fine washables market niche. Although its product, Handle with Care, offered secondary product advantages, consumers still preferred Woolite on the primary cleaning dimension. Despite millions in marketing expenditures, the product failed to establish itself with consumers.

Another current example of a would-be niche brand that is foundering because it lacks a meaningful product difference is SOS Glassworks. In order to crack into the glass cleaning niche, Miles Laboratories was banking on the equity of the SOS brand name. But without performance superiority, the SOS brand name is proving to be inadequate. At this point Windex is beating back this competitive challenge with ease.

Likewise in the mildew stain remover niche of the household cleaning category, a brand called X-14 is attacking the niche leader, Tilex. While X-14 is technically stronger, the majority of consumers still prefer the overall performance of Tilex. As such, it is doubtful that X-14 will ever loosen Tilex's grip on this niche market.

NO CONSUMER DEMAND

To parody the old adage, "What's not worth doing is not worth doing well!" No matter how good a niche product may be, it can't succeed if there's insufficient consumer demand. Inspired by the enormous popularity of Mexican/southwest regional specialty foods, several major marketers predicted that Cajun Cuisine would be the next big regional hit. But nationwide the consumer demand simply was not there. After a series of unsuccessful product introductions, Cajun cuisine, at least for the present, has faded from the food scene.

In the home cleaning category, Dow recently introduced a line of impregnated towels called Spiffits. Clearly the product offers the added convenience of one-step cleaning. But Spiffits is significantly more expensive than other spray cleaner alternatives. In view of Spiffits' premium pricing, it is unlikely that there will be adequate consumer demand to support this niche product long term.

In the food segment Campbell's has been unsuccessful to date in establishing a new niche of refrigerated products with its Fresh Chef salad line. While this project has experienced many technical difficulties, the underlying problem appears to be a lack of consumer demand. With fresh salad ingredients readily available, consumers appear to be disinterested or unwilling to pay a premium price for this product.

POOR PRODUCT PERFORMANCE

Based on the growing health and fitness consciousness among American consumers, there is no question that nonalcoholic beer is an extremely viable niche product opportunity. But to date, no company has been able to brew a nonalcoholic beer with a taste comparable to its alcoholic counterparts. As a result there have been a number of tepid introductions, such as Moussy, and this niche has yet to be firmly established.

One of Johnson & Johnson's few failures in the health care category has been Medipren. Introduced in the late 80s, this pain reliever attempted to create a new niche in the analgesic market—a specialized product for aches and pains. The problem was that Medipren's formula did not deliver superior performance against this promise. Its ingredients were the same as a number of other analgesic brands; therefore, consumers did not notice a significant difference in pain relief. While "aches and pains" may represent a legitimate market niche, Medipren does not appear to have the pain-relieving horsepower required to capitalize on this opportunity.

RANGE OF ACTIVITY

The case histories and examples cited in this chapter provide a glimpse of the vast range of niche marketing activities currently in progress throughout the American marketplace. Niche marketing in its many forms offers smaller marketers the antidote for the growing power and influence of the megabrands. The potential for niche products is almost unlimited. The only restraints will be the ever-changing needs of consumers and the level of imagination that niche marketers can apply to the task.

NOTES

1. Pamela Ellis-Simons, "One from the Heart," *Marketing & Media Decisions*, March 1990, p. 32.
2. David Wellman, "Healthy Choice Moves Out," *Food & Beverage Marketing*, March 1990, p. 31.
3. Sandra D. Atchison, "Why Celestial Seasonings Wasn't Kraft's Cup of Tea," *Business Week*, May 8, 1989, p. 76.
4. "A National Mop-up for Murphy's Oil Soap," Marketing Week, *Adweek*, November 26, 1990, p. 21.
5. Ibid.
6. Ibid.
7. Tony Dela Cruz, "Motorized Toothbrushes Trimming Tags," *HFD*, March 19, 1990, p. 60.
8. Carol Carr, "Bausch & Lomb to Promote Accessories for Interplak," Retailing home furnishings, *HFD*, December 18, 1989, p. 60.
9. Jennifer Lawrence, "P&G's Metamucil Plan Broadens," *Advertising Age*, April 8, 1991, p. 1.
10. David Kiley, "Scott Throws in Advertising Towel," Marketing Week, *Adweek*, March 7, 1988, p. 1.
11. George Lazarus, "Scott Rolling Out a Megapitch Here," *Chicago Tribune*, October 15, 1990, sec. 4.

PART 4

MEGABRANDS AND THE FUTURE

Chapter Twelve
Megabrands and the Future

In 1968 a previously unseen image captured the imagination of people around the world. The photo, taken by Apollo astronauts as they orbited the moon, depicted the beautiful blue orb of the earth rising above the barren lunar landscape. Dubbed "Earthrise," the photograph quickly came to symbolize the oneness and interdependency of all the nations and peoples on earth.

Like most artistic insights, the vision of that photograph has yet to be fully realized. But indisputably, since the day it was snapped, the same technology that catapulted men to the moon has been bringing our world closer together. In science, in manufacturing, and in marketing, the boundaries that once separated nations are blurring and beginning to disappear. A true, global economy that recognizes no borders is emerging. As we approach the year 2000, many more American companies and products will be performing in an international arena.

This transformation is already well on its way. As Japanese management consultant Kenichi Ohmae has observed, "On a political map, the boundaries between countries are as clear as ever. But on a competitive map, a map showing the real flows of financial and industrial activity, these boundaries have largely disappeared. What has eaten them away is the persistent, ever speedier flow of information."[1]

Within the U.S. marketplace, many Americans are poignantly aware of the presence of foreign products, most notably

Japanese, in the automotive and consumer electronics sectors. But most are not nearly as mindful of the position of foreign companies in America's consumer products categories. Yet in these categories too, offshore corporations are well-established and growing.

MULTINATIONAL COMPETITORS

Within the U.S. food and household product categories, foreign-owned multinational companies like Nestle and Unilever have long been major factors. These companies have employed a decentralized management approach with strong domestic management teams to build thriving U.S. businesses. More recently the British conglomerate Grand Metropolitan became a major player in the U.S. food industry with its acquisition of Pillsbury. In the pharmaceutical industry, the German drug manufacturer Bayer acquired Miles Laboratories in the early 1980s. Likewise, a French company, Rhone-Poulenc, assumed a controlling interest in a drug company, Rorer.

In addition to direct ownership, many major U.S. companies have swapped stock and formed "strategic alliances" with foreign companies in similar businesses. For example, the Clorox Company has formed a strategic alliance with the huge German household products company, Henkel. Then, too, there are the many imported products, such as Heineken beer and Perrier bottled water, that have captured large shares of U.S. domestic markets.

Today the average U.S. consumer's favorable experience with foreign brands is starting to break down the traditional American preference for American-made goods. According to a recent Roper survey, Americans still have a predisposition to "buy American"—all things being equal (e.g., price, quality, etc.). However, if a foreign product is superior on any key dimension, most U.S. consumers have no problem purchasing the foreign-made product.

The survey observes,

The main point is that the traditional advantage U.S. manufacturers have held simply by being American is irrevocably eroding. American consumers have become global shoppers: Increasingly, they want to buy brands they perceive as being the best for the money, regardless of the country of origin. Under these new rules, it's more important for domestic brands to be associated with the words "quality" and "value" than with the phrase, "made in the USA."[2]

NEW-PRODUCT SOURCE

Unlike their foreign competitors, most major American packaged goods companies have only begun to aggressively market their major brands outside the United States. Within the past 10 years, as growth in domestic markets has slowed, these companies have looked offshore for more robust markets for their products. However, despite their historical focus on the primary domestic market, many of these same U.S. companies have long considered international markets, particularly in Europe, to be important sources for new American products.

A recent article explains,

"Most big companies now are systematically scanning the world for new product ideas," says Marc Particelli, a senior vice president with the consulting firm Booze-Allen & Hamilton Inc. in New York. Elizabeth Harrington, corporate director of consumer products marketing for A.T. Kearney, Inc., a Chicago consulting firm, adds, "More companies are saying, 'Instead of spending all this money on research and development, let's go to the treasure trove in Europe and Asia.'"

Marketers can reduce their risk by importing product ideas that dovetail with trends in the U.S. After studying Europe's muesli cereals—based on a mixture of fruit, grains and nuts invented in Switzerland—Kellogg rolled out in the U.S. its Mueslix brand, one of its most successful cereal introductions in years.[3]

Today the realities of a global economy are causing American manufacturers to concentrate enormous energy and resources on the development of international markets. As they do this, the concept of the megabrand is taking on a whole new dimension of meaning. In the future these giant brands will not only dominate national markets but international markets as well. They will be-

come the favorite products of shoppers in the countless retail outlets throughout the global village.

EUROPE 1992

In their international operations most corporations tend to consider the global market in terms of three huge trading blocks:
North America, Europe, and Asia. With the impending creation
of a single European economic community, the eyes of most
American corporations are turned toward Europe. In 1992 the
markets of the 12 members of the European Economic Community will be unified, creating the world's richest single trading
area, with over 325 million consumers. Trade barriers will be eliminated and national regulations regarding both advertising and
product standards will be brought into sync. Thus, in one fell
swoop a market that is larger and more prosperous than the
United States will be created.

In the past major marketers have tended to approach each
European country separately because of massive differences in
national policies and business conditions. In many instances this
meant marketing the identical product under different brand
names in every country. Now, in preparation for the unification,
many consumer products companies are moving to develop pan-
continental "Eurobrands."

According to *The New York Times*,

> Scores of companies are creating "Eurobrands," giving products a
> single brand name throughout most or all of Europe. Many are
> supporting their products with "Euro-ads"—advertisements that
> except for the language are similar in message and often identical
> or nearly identical in execution.
>
> For instance, in Britain and France, Mars, Inc., the United States
> candy maker, has already changed the name of its Treets candies to
> M&M's, the name it uses in the United States. Over the next five
> years, Nestle S.A., the giant Swiss foods company, plans to replace
> several national brands it uses to sell cheese in Europe with the
> Nestle brand name.
>
> And Colgate-Palmolive Company, the big United States con-
> sumer products maker, has reduced the number of Palmolive

soaps it sells in Europe to only three fragrances, down from at least 10 a short time ago.[4]

Common Advertising

Marketers recognize that unification certainly will not do away with all national differences. But even in situations where identical products must still be sold under different brand names, companies are seeking closer coordination of marketing activities across countries. One of the principal means of achieving this coordination is the creation of a consistent look in all pan-European marketing communications, from product packaging through advertising.

Advertising in particular can be especially effective in forging a shared identity. Recently a number of major marketers have begun to produce single campaigns designed for many countries. In addition to the obvious marketing benefits, these so-called Euro-ads offer companies two additional advantages:

1. They permit ad agencies to concentrate their attention on creating the single most effective advertising format, instead of diluting their energies across many, different executions.
2. The Euro-ad approach is far more cost effective, since each separate commercial can cost up to $200,000 to produce.

However, despite their many advantages, Euro-ads are not destined to be universally applied in the foreseeable future. In many situations cultural differences make it impossible to create a single ad that works well in every European nation. According to a recent report,

Experts say advertisements that focus on specific styles of life travel least well from country to country, while those that travel best demonstrate a product's effectiveness, like the strength of a glue, or that rely on universal values, like love of family, friendship, and social harmony. Some companies still use two or three basic advertisements to address the cultural differences, which is a big difference from the dozen or more they once used.[5]

Shared Media

The growth of Euro-advertising is also being stimulated by the emergence of new, pan-European media forms. By some estimates, one third of European homes will be receiving satellite channels by 1992. In addition, new continentwide publications, such as Robert Maxwell's newspaper, *The European*, are beginning to appear. The new media channels offer marketers the opportunity to communicate a Euro-ad message more simply and efficiently than the historical approach of piecing together a media plan on a country-by-country basis.

By mid-decade the unification of the European market will be well in place. Currently, additional western European nations are negotiating to become members of this economic community. Longer-term, the former communist block nations of eastern Europe will become full trading partners, swelling the consumer ranks and buying power even further. For megabrand marketers in the United States and around the world, a unified Europe will be a primary growth target for many years to come.

As the attention of American managers shifts increasingly to the European scene, the management and marketing activities of major American brands and their European variants will move closer and closer together. As this happens, the identities of a growing number of American brands and Eurobrands will merge and an increasing number of products will move into the ranks of true, international megabrands.

ASIA

Historically American marketers have had a much more difficult time establishing U.S. brand names in major Asian markets. While the United States shares many cultural roots with western Europe, there are fewer strong cultural ties between the United States and Asian nations. As a result most American companies entering Asia are moving into alien territory. Before they can hope to succeed in these unfamiliar markets, they must make a serious effort to understand each country's culture, consumers, and business practices.

Japan

Nowhere is this challenge more formidable than in Asia's largest market—Japan. Japan's trade restrictions, negotiating etiquette, and distribution channels make the marketing of American brands particularly difficult. Nonetheless, resourceful American consumer product marketers have overcome these odds and made substantial inroads. Procter & Gamble provides one example of a Japanese success story.

In fiscal 1990 P&G registered sales of $1 billion in Japan. However, the company's success did not come easily. Procter's Japanese enterprise lost money from the time the company entered the market in 1973 until 1987. According to P&G Chairman-CEO Edwin L. Artzt, "P&G stormed into the Japanese market with American products, American advertising, and American sales methods and promotional strategies."[6] The results were disastrous until the company learned to adapt its products and marketing style to the Japanese culture.

P&G now sells more than 20 products in Japan, including the number-one brand in seven consumer product categories. According to Chairman Artzt, "You must know your customers, the trade, the culture, and your competition well enough to think and act like a Japanese company."[7] Some of Procter's U.S. megabrands, most notably Pampers, have succeeded with their U.S. brand names. Others like Always feminine protection products and Pert shampoo are marketed under different brand names. But in every instance the products and marketing programs have been specifically tailored to the Japanese market.

Warner-Lambert's Schick razors is another U.S. brand that has been tremendously successful in Japan by tailoring its products and marketing programs to the specific needs of the Japanese market. Today Schick holds a 60 percent share of market compared to only 10 percent for Gillette. While Gillette has favored an American approach to marketing, Schick has remained strongly Japanese focused. As a Schick manager put it, "Schick hasn't used a foreigner in ads in the past six years."[8]

Coca-Cola is another American marketer whose business is thriving in Asia. Coke has been doing business in Asia since the 1920s, and its success is based on an indepth knowledge of Asian markets. According to consultant Kenichi Ohmae,

Coke has 70 percent of the Japanese market for soft drinks. The reason is that Coke took the time and made the investment to build up a full range of local functional strengths, particularly in its route sales force and franchised vending machines.

It is, after all, the Coke van or truck that replaces empty bottles with new ones, not the trucks of independent wholesalers or distributors. When Coke first moved into Japan, it did not understand the complex, many-layered distribution system for such products. So it used the capital of local bottlers to recreate the kind of sales force it has used so well in the United States. This represented a heavy, front-end investment, but it has paid off handsomely. Coke redefined the domestic game in Japan—and it did so, not from a distance, but with a deliberate "insiderization" of functional strengths.[9]

China

Not only does Coke enjoy a massive business in Japan, the brand is also number one in Hong Kong and Taiwan. Now Coke is beginning to build a significant business in mainland China. In addition to its cola brands, Coke is applying its knowledge of national markets to develop and sell other soft drinks designed to specifically meet local tastes.

A recent article stated,

Besides selling its colas and Fanta and Hi-C fruit-flavored drinks, Coke is trying to grab even more market share with a line of Chinese-style favorites such as soy milk and flavored tea drinks. It also wants to boost soft drink consumption, still only a quarter of U.S. levels. . . . It may be years before the market is rich enough to pay off for either Coke or Pepsi. But with 1.1 billion potential customers at stake, the Cola Wars have broken out in earnest in China.[10]

GLOBAL MEGABRANDS

By the beginning of this decade, a select group of international megabrands had already spread their marketing web across North America, Europe, and Asia. Remarkably, many of America's largest consumer products companies were already doing a

third or more of their total sales volume in international markets.
The table below lists 1989 international sales for five of the largest
packaged goods marketers in the United States:

1989 International Sales

	($ Billions)	% of Worldwide Volume
Procter & Gamble	9.1	30
Kellogg	1.7	37
Warner-Lambert	1.9	46
Johnson & Johnson	4.9	50
Coca-Cola	4.9	55

Source: "100 Leading National Advertisers," *Advertising Age*, September 26, 1990, p. 6.

In the future it is clear that megabrands will move even more
forcefully into the global arena. While marketers of these products will have to respect national differences in their worldwide
marketing efforts, the efficiencies and synergies that these megabrands will enjoy due to their international presence will endow
many with world-class marketing clout. And as the business
world continues to shrink, the influence of these products will
continue to grow.

GLOBAL PRODUCT STANDARDIZATION

Within the marketing community a debate is taking place about
how standardized megabrand product lines and marketing programs can truly become as they move into the global marketplace.
Most experts agree that significant levels of standardization are
possible. However, many also believe that national marketers
must always be given the flexibility to adapt products and programs to the needs of local consumers and market conditions.

Many thinkers, including Professor Theodore Levitt of the
Harvard Business School, are convinced that differences among
nations will diminish and eventually disappear as the world
evolves towards a true global community. Levitt states,

Everywhere everything gets more like everything else, as the
world's preference structure gets pressed into homogenized commonality.

Ancient differences in national tastes and preferences, in modes of doing business and the institutions of commerce, fall before the homogenizing modernity everybody experiences via the new technological facilitators. The global commonality of what's preferred leads inescapably to the global standardization of products, of manufacturing, and the institutions of trade and commerce. Small nation-based markets are transmogrified and expanded into large global-sized markets, with accompanying economies of scale in production, distribution, marketing, and management.

. . . This converges finally into world-standardized product lines that compete on the basis of appropriate value—the best combination of price, quality, reliability, and delivery for products that, in respect to design, functionality, and even fashionability, are globally identical.[11]

It appears that Levitt's global perspective is beginning to win new converts among large international advertisers. Global advertising, originally dismissed by many as inappropriate, appears to be gaining new credibility. *Ad Age* reports, "This summer (1991), marketers of products from liquor to computers have unveiled ambitious global efforts backed by big budgets. Among the newcomers: Merrill Lynch & Company, Joseph E. Seagram & Sons, Digital Equipment Corp., Xerox Corporation and Chase Manhattan Bank."[12]

Most experts believe that the best candidates for global advertising campaigns are high-tech products, fashion items, and other products that are sold primarily on image. In many of these cases, it appears that consumers around the world "speak the same language" and therefore can be persuaded by common communications approaches.

MEGABRANDS ON THE HOME FRONT

In the coming years megabrands will also continue to expand their influence here on the home front. The domestic marketplace forces that fostered the strategy of growth through line extension will intensify through the remainder of the decade. Economies of scale in manufacturing, marketing, and information technology will grow more pronounced, making it more difficult for new brands to successfully compete. Likewise, the consolidation of power in the retail trade as well as media fragmentation will continue unabated, making it increasingly difficult for new brands to gain retail distribution and generate consumer awareness and trial.

Emphasis on Line Extension

As a result, the current preference of major marketers in favor of line extensions over new products will rise above the 1990s' high water mark in the future. According to a recent industry report, "Marketers leaned heavily on established brand names when launching new products in 1990. Fully 63 percent of all introductions were line extensions—either new varieties, formulations, or sizes. Less than 20 percent of new products were launched under an entirely new brand name."[13]

Through 1995 the ratio of line extensions to new products is projected to become even more lopsided, as evidenced by the results of another recent survey. In this study, "76 percent of marketers forecasted that 70 percent or more of their new products in the next five years would be line extensions."[14] In a marketplace with such a line extension orientation, the advantages and economies of scale that megabrands enjoy will become further exaggerated.

Shorter New-Product Life Cycles

Another market factor working against new products and in favor of large extended lines is the pace of change itself. Over the past three decades, researchers have observed that the product life cycle of new brands is growing shorter. While the causes of this phenomenon are not entirely clear, it seems reasonable to speculate that the constant pressure of competitive innovation makes it very difficult for most new brands to establish deep roots in the marketplace. The competitive counterattacks of the modern-day market do not allow most new brands to establish solid, lasting consumer relationships.

The phenomenon of shorter new-product life cycles was recently cited by *New Product News*, an industry publication that has been tracking major packaged goods new-product trends since 1964. In their 25th anniversary special report, the editors observed, "In spite of the staying power of older brands, newer products face increasingly short life cycles. Food fads have produced short-range phenomena, such as Pop Rocks and Wine Coolers. Categories such as frozen yogurt and alcohol-free beer appear to have died and then reappear in more successful formulations. Few brands actually die violent deaths . . . they just slowly fade away."[15]

MARKETING IN THE NEXT MILLENNIUM

As we approach the year 2000, the growth of extended mega-brand lines will also be stimulated by advances in computer and communications technology. These advances will allow marketers to target individual consumers and develop products and programs that address their specific needs far more precisely than they can today. At the core of all this activity will be sophisticated computer database capabilities. In the world of marketing, the computer revolution may have begun in the 80s, but it will come to full fruition in the 90s.

Hypertargeting

In the years ahead, targeting of audiences will be replaced by hypertargeting of smaller groups within these standard groups. As described in a recent article, "The key to hypertargeting is to split the atom. In the mid-90s, we'll be splitting each group again and again. As each group becomes smaller and smaller, we'll still be able to fine-tune the same (even more specific) offer within each subgroup."[16]

In the area of direct mail, hypertargeting will result in significant improvements in response rates and major reductions in waste. As predicted by the same author, "21st century direct mail will demand a huge decrease in the number of pieces mailed and a huge increase in the percentage of response."[17] But hypertargeting will not only be limited to direct mail. Advances in communications technology will make television and all existing media more selective and will introduce entirely new forms of targeted media vehicles.

Selective Media

Experts predict that there will be an explosion in the number of cable TV channels during the next 10 years. This proliferation of channels and their specific programming will allow marketers to more selectively reach particular target groups. According to the *New York Times,*

> Advances in video technology are likely to transform the television landscape over the next several years, expanding the number of channels available on cable systems to as many as 300 from an average of 33 today.
>
> . . . The expansion of cable channels to 5 to 10 times their current number is widely accepted as realistic by cable and network executives, given such developments in fiber-optic cable and digital video compression, both of which allow many more channels to be delivered to homes.[18]

Over the next few years, fiber optics and computer technology will also make interactive television a reality. Interactive TV will allow marketers to establish a dialogue with consumers in real time and help them personalize their product messages to a degree never before possible. By some estimates 80 percent of U.S. homes will be wired for interactive television by the turn of the century.

Finally, entirely new forms of media will emerge that will allow sophisticated megabrand marketers to get their messages to consumers in a personalized, high-impact manner. For example, 7 percent of the total U.S. adult population now uses a fax machine on a typical day. As fax machines become more pervasive, marketers will be able to instantaneously transmit customized messages to consumers. If used in a responsible manner, this capability could allow megabrand marketers to have a direct line into their customers' homes.

Selective Promotion

In the promotional area, computer technology will permit megabrand marketers to move from regional promotions to true neighborhood promotions. In discussing a recent new line extension launch by Frito-Lay, *Ad Age* said,

> Frito-Lay is hitting the neighborhoods, taking its regional market-ing strategy one step futher.
>
> When Frito-Lay starts rolling out its light product line, the com-pany will pay special attention to sales in selected supermarkets—stores identified through a sophisticated computerized database as likely to rack up higher sales for Chee-Tos Light, Doritos Light, and Ruffles Light. . . .
>
> Working with Market Metrics, a consultancy, Frito has identi-fied individual supermarkets whose customers match the demo-graphics of the light line. The Frito sales force then stresses to the retailer the match between the store's shopper profile and the product line demographics. . . . Matching individual stores with the products also enabled Frito to increase promotional spending in key neighborhoods early in the introduction.[19]

Obviously these technological breakthroughs and targeted marketing techniques will be available to all marketers. But only the megabrands will have the financial resources necessary to stay at the cutting edge of these developments and to quickly im-plement new approaches on a broad, national scale. In most cases smaller competitors will find themselves a few important steps behind.

Product Technology

Finally as product technology advances, major marketers will be most likely to apply scientific breakthroughs to their established megabrand lines, not new products, in order to provide these crit-ical businesses with significant points of differentiation. In major categories, smaller brands will find it extremely difficult to com-pete in a cost-effective manner against the technological prowess of the megabrands. As the pace of technological change quickens, many of these smaller product lines will be left in the dust.

In the coming decade, mass customization will be the hall-mark of megabrand marketing. Domestically product lines will continue to proliferate as new line items are introduced that pro-vide customized benefits for smaller groups of target consumers.

On the international front mass customization will be utilized to adapt the same basic products for consumers in different countries around the world. Consistent with the concept of the megabrand, all of these products will provide variations of the same core benefit.

In short, those who long to return to the single-focus simplicity of marketing's good old days will be sorely disappointed as the 90s move forward. As FCB's Laurel Cutler insightfully remarked,

> Everyone thinks of a 'brand' as a noun, as static, stationary, and stable. I believe in the 90s we've got to start thinking of 'brand' as a verb. We've got to think of it as branding—something that's active, moving, and evolving."

Today, there's little doubt that constant, accelerating change in major brand lines is a fact of life that's here to stay.

FROM GLOBAL TO PERSONAL

By the year 2000 megabrand management will be entirely computer-driven. On a desktop computer monitor, the brand manager of the future will be able to call up information as vast as worldwide sales and profits or as particular as the sales of one line item in a neighborhood grocery store. He or she will be able to instantaneously access consumer data as general as target audience demographics or as specific as the purchase behavior of a single person. Through computer-modeling techniques, a brand manager will be able to vary every element of the marketing mix and test the impact of these alternative scenarios on worldwide sales or the sales of a single consumer.

As the 1990s progress, the business of marketing will seem a Zen-like riddle: It will be at the same time both global and personal, both large and small. Computers will alow managers to organize and manipulate vast quantities of information on both the macro and the micro levels. But as is the case today, the computer will remain a tool that can accomplish nothing until put to work by an experienced individual.

THE NEW REALITY

Paradoxically, as the science of marketing becomes more powerful, so too does the need for the art of marketing, that is to say, the marketing imagination of the individual manager. For in the end, the same technologies will be available to each major competitor. Only those companies that stay focused on the individual consumer and whose corporate culture fosters and rewards individual innovation will be able to build and maintain market-dominating megabrands.

In the vast complexity of the modern world, it's easy to minimize the importance of individuals and to view all parts as interchangeable. But the most advanced research in molecular biology is now suggesting that the action of the tiniest component on the DNA strand could well mean the difference between normal, healthy growth and cancer. In the future world of global megabrands, the quality of the thinking and leadership of individual managers will ultimately spell the difference in the competition between huge, global brands.

By the late 1990s, the national sales maps that have traditionally hung in offices of marketing managers will be replaced by new images of the vast, global marketplace. But even in this huge, global context, the success or failure of products and corporations will still hinge on the work of individual managers directed at individual consumers. Only those companies that stay focused on this "individual" reality will be consistently successful in developing their products, implementing their programs, and most importantly, inspiring and motivating their people.

NOTES

1. Kenichi Ohmae, "Managing in a Borderless World," *Harvard Business Review*, May/June 1989, p. 152.
2. "Today's Global Shopper," *The Public Pulse*, October 1990, p. 2.
3. Michael J. McCarthy, "U.S. Companies Shop Abroad for Product Ideas," *The Wall Street Journal*, March 14, 1990, p. B1.
4. Steven Prokesch, "Eurosell Pervades the Continent," *The New York Times*, May 31, 1990, p. C1.
5. Ibid., p. C2.

6. Laurie Freeman, "Japan Rises to P&G's No. 3 Market," *Advertising Age*, December 10, 1990, p. 42.

7. Ibid.

8. Yukimo Ono, "Gillette Tries to Nick Schick in Japan," *The Wall Street Journal*, February 4, 1991, p. B1.

9. Kenichi Ohmae, "Managing in a Borderless World," *Harvard Business Review*, May/June 1989, p. 152.

10. Pete Engardio, "In Asia, the Sweet Taste of Success," *Business Week*, November 26, 1990, p. 96.

11. Theodore Levitt, *The Marketing Imagination*, (New York: The Free Press, 1983), p. 24.

12. Gary Levin, "Ads Going Global," *Advertising Age*, July 22, 1991, p. 4.

13. "Year of the New Product," *Food & Beverage Marketing*, March 1991, p. 14.

14. Edward F. Ogiba, "Dark Days for New Products," *Food & Beverage Marketing*, December 1989, p. 21.

15. Martin Friedman, "98,900 New Products Later," *New Product News*, April 8, 1990, p. 14.

16. Carol Nelson, "Squeezing Out That Extra Drop of Response," *Direct Marketing*, April 1990, p. 46.

17. Ibid., p. 48.

18. Bill Carter, "Brave New TV World," *The New York Times*, May 13, 1991, p. C1.

19. Jennifer Lawrence, "Frito's Micro Move," *Advertising Age*, February 12, 1990, p. 44.

20. Raymond Serafin, "Blasting through Ad Clutter: Carmakers Finding There's More than TV to Draw Consumers," *Advertising Age*, January 22, 1990, p. S-1.

Index

A

Advertising; *see also* Media
for Alka-Seltzer and Rolaids, 143–44
for Barbasol, 193–94
for Campbell's, 135–37
for Clorox, 137–39
consumers' reactions to, 33–34, 69–70
emotion in, 67–70, 72–73
in Europe, 207–8
fragmentation of, 22–25
for Jell-O, 132
for Lysol, 130
for niche products, 173–74
for a product line, 49–51, 103–7, 120
for ScotTowels, 195–96
for Tide, 140–41
for Tylenol, 141–42
unique selling proposition, 63–65
Aesthetic variations, 88–89
Alka-Seltzer (case study), 143–44
American Express, 66–67
Anacin, 16
Arm & Hammer, 52, 164
Asia, marketing in, 208–10
Asian-Americans, marketing to, 114–15

B

Baby boom, 11, 82
Ban (antiperspirant), 99
case study, 144–46
Barbasol (case study), 193–94
Bausch & Lomb, 191
Benefit variations; *see* Product benefits
Brand character and symbols, 74–75
Brand dominance, 39–40
Brand equity, 6–10
Brand image, 43–44, 46–47
Brand naming, 167
Brand switching, 48
Brands; *see* Megabrands
Bufferin, 16

C

Cajun cuisine, 197–98
California, niche marketing in, 158–59
California Raisins, 75
Campbell's, 44, 47, 184–85, 198
case study, 135–37
Cannibalization, 48
Catalog marketing, 162
Category extensions, 51–53
Category manager, 118–19
Celestial Seasonings (case study), 187–88

Clorox, 49, 156; *see also* Tilex
    case study, 137–39
Clorox-2, 69
Coca-Cola, 47, 98, 209–10
    case study, 134–35
Colgate, 132
Competitive threats to brands, 78–80
Complementary marketing, 44–45
Concept/product testing, 90–91
Consumer attitudes, 84–86
Consumer promotion, 105–6
Crest, 41, 50
    case study, 132–34
Customization of products, 216–17
Customized marketing, 113–16

D

Datril, 43
Davidson, J. Hugh, 12–13
Demographic trends, 81–83
Diet Coke, 98, 134
Distribution channels in niche market-
    ing, 159–62, 190–93
Dreft, 175–76
Drucker, Peter, 81–82

E

Economy of scale, 20–29
Emotional benefits, 64–70, 72–73, 130,
    131–32
Endorsements, 176
Environmental concerns of
    consumers, 85–86
Europe, marketing to, 206–8
Excedrin, 16, 58

F

Failure fee, 28
Farquhar, Peter H., 6–9
FCB grid, 63
Form of products, variations in, 89–90
Formula variations, 87–88

Frame of reference, 60–61
Frito-Lay, 31–32, 216
Future shock, 32–36
Future value of brand equity, 9

G–H

Gillette, 209
Halo effect, 104–5, 120
    for Tylenol, 142
    for Campbell's, 137
Handle with Care (laundry soap), 197
Healthy Choice (case study), 184–85
Hispanics, marketing to, 114
Holistic approach to marketing, 95–
    96, 104
Hypertargeting, 214; *see also* Micro-
    marketing

I

Image Configurations, 67
Incremental sales, 48–49
Information overload, 33–34
Information technology in retailing,
    29–32
Interplak, 176

J–K

Jell-O, 51
    case study, 131–32
K.C. Masterpiece, 158
Kellogg, 205

L

Leveraging, 94–109, 135–39
Life-style of consumers, 83–84, 92
Lifetime value, 125
Light, Larry, 39–40
Line extensions, 18–19, 41–53
    of Alka-Seltzer, 143–44
    of Ban, 145
    brand equity and, 9–10

Line extensions—*Cont.*
  of Clorox, 138–39
  of Coca-Cola, 134–35
  of Crest, 133
  developing, 77–93
  future, 213
  introducing new items, 102–8
  leveraging spending on, 94–109
  major versus minor, 96–99
  micromarketing, 111–16
  and positioning, 58–59
  of Tide, 139–41
Lister, John, 123
Listerine, 61
Lysol (case study), 129–31

M

McQueen, Josh, 64–65
Market fragmentation, 17
Marketing; *see also* Megabrands;
    Micromarketing; Niche market-
    ing; Relationship marketing
  future of, 203–18
  of megabrands, 38–53
  of niche products, 166–81
  plan, executing, 110–26
  plan for Tide, 139–41
  plan for Tylenol, 141–42
Market maturation, 11–12
Market segmentation, 15–17
Market share, 39–40
Market target, 60–61
Media; *see also* Advertising
  customizing, for micromarketing,
    112–13
  in Europe, 208
  fragmentation of, 22–25
  future of, 215
  use of, for niche products, 169–71
Media content analysis, 92–93
Media flighting, 121–22
Medipren, 198
Megabrands; *see also* Line extensions
  case studies, 128–46

Megabrands—*Cont.*
  competitive threats to, 78–80
  defined, xvii, 39
  future of, 203–18
  and global market, 203–12
  line extensions, 41–53, 77–98
  marketing of, 38–53, 110–26, 152–
    54
  positioning, 57–76
  reasons for rise of, 20–36
Mennen, 145–46
Mergers and acquisitions, 4–6, 177
Merriam, John, 92–93
Metamucil (case study), 191–93
Micromarketing, 31–32, 111–16, 214–
  18
Modeling of product line budgets, 102
Multinational corporations, 204–5
Murphy's Oil Soap, 156
  case study, 188–90
Music in advertising, 68–69

N

Need gap analysis, 15–16
New mothers, marketing to, 114–15
Niche marketing, 149–99
  case studies, 183–99
  versus megabrand marketing, 152–
    54
  product development, 151–65
Nontraditional media, 171
Nyquil, 61

O

Ohmae, Kenichi, 203, 210
Orelia (Orangina), 157
Organization, marketing, 117–19, 166,
  176–81
Osborne, Thomas, 158–59

P

Packaging, 123–24
Pain reliever market, 16

Parity products, 14–15
Pepsi, 134
Planters, 51
Pledge, 65
Point of difference, 60–62; see also
    Product benefits
Positioning, 57–76
    of Ban, 144–46
    of Healthy Choice, 184–85
    of Jell-O, 131–32
    of Lysol, 129–31
    of Metamucil, 192–93
    of Murphy's Oil Soap, 189–90
    of niche products, 154–57
    of product lines, 96
    of Tilex, 185–87
Present value of brand equity, 8–9
Price/value advertising, 174
Pricing of niche products, 167–69
Procter & Gamble, 209; see also Crest;
    Dreft; Metamucil; Tide
Product benefits, 42–43, 50–51, 62–73;
    see also Emotional benefits; Point
    of difference; Rational benefits
Product development
    of megabrands, 77–93
    in niche marketing, 151–65
Product differentiation, 197, 216–17;
    see also Line extensions
Product life cycle, 52–53, 213–
    14
Product lines; see Line extensions
Product performance, 12–15
Product standardization, global, 211–
    12
Promotion of product lines, 25–29,
    122–23
    to consumers, 105–6
    in the future, 215–16
    of niche products, 174–76
    to professionals, 160–61, 172–73
    trade, 106
Public relations in niche marketing,
    173
Purex, 137

Q–R

Qualitative testing, 90
Rational benefits, 62–64, 70–72, 129–
    30, 131
Regional marketing, 157–59, 187–90
Regional media, 170–71
Relationship marketing, 125–26, 172–
    73
Retail promotion, 26–29
Rolaids, 143–44

S

Sales promotion, 25–29
Sampling, 175
Schick, 209
Science Diet, 161
ScotTowels (case study), 195–96
Secret (antiperspirant), 61
Slim-Fast, 68
Slotting allowance, 27–28
SOS Glassworks, 197
Spending; see Advertising; Leveraging
Spiffits, 198
Stouffer's, 184–85
Strategic business units, 117–19, 166
Suave (shampoo), 163–64
Super Bowl, 23, 26

T

Targeted media, 169–70
Technology and product differen-
    tiation, 216–17
Testing of new products, 90–91
Tide, 42–43, 49
    case study, 139–41
Tilex, 156, 197; see also Clorox
    case study, 185–87
Timing in advertising, 106–7
Trade allowances, 26
Trade promotion, 106

Training programs for niche market-
    ing, 181
Tylenol, 16, 42–43, 67–68, 71–73
    case study, 141–42

U–V

Unique selling proposition, 63–65
Value pricing, 162–65, 193–96
Vaseline, 41

Vaughn, Dick, 63, 65
Venture groups, 178–80

W–Z

Windex, 58, 197
Wisk, 79–80
Woolite, 197
X-14, 197
Yankelovich Monitor, 84, 164
Zero-based budgeting, 99–102

OTHER BUSINESS ONE IRWIN TITLES OF INTEREST TO YOU

MARKETING TO HOME-BASED BUSINESSES
Jeffrey P. Davidson

With a median income of $47,000, work-at-homers are a market niche with plenty of money to spend. More than three fourths of home-based entrepreneurs are married, and 72 percent have children. Davidson helps you tap this affluent, fast-growing market and acquire the knowledge, strategies, and techniques to effectively market to home-based businesses.
ISBN: 1-55623-475-9 $39.95

A Maxwell Sroge Report
THE UNITED STATES MAIL ORDER INDUSTRY

Whether you're a direct marketing professional, an investor, or an entrepreneur, Sroge helps you find profitable market niches by analyzing both the existing and the developing mail order marketplace. Use the information to project probable growth patterns and to allocate valuable marketing resources more accurately.
ISBN: 1-55623-486-4 $55.00

CREATING DEMAND
Powerful Tips and Tactics for Marketing Your Product or Service
Richard Ott

Richard Ott goes way beyond the "4 Ps" and explains the real demand-building process. He shows you how to set the stage for success, how to leverage demand to peak levels, and how to sustain it. He explains how person-to-person influence actually works and how you can tap into the tremendous power of human influence to affect the masses—and cause demand to erupt!
ISBN: 1-55623-560-7 $27.50

SELLING TO THE AFFLUENT
The Professional's Guide to Closing the Sales that Count
Dr. Thomas Stanley

Improve your closing percentage . . . and income. Dr. Stanley shows you how to approach wealthy prospects at the moment they are most likely to buy. In Marketing to the Affluent, Stanley told you how to find them. Now he tells you how to sell them.
ISBN: 1-55623-418-X $55.00

MARKETING TO THE AFFLUENT
Dr. Thomas Stanley

A 1989 business book award finalist! Dr. Stanley shows you how to get the true demographics, psychographics, and buying and patronage habits of the wealthy. Includes in-depth interviews with some of the nation's top sales and marketing professionals to help you pinpoint your best prospects.
ISBN: 1-55623-105-9 $55.00

NICHE SELLING
How to Find Your Customer in a Crowded Market
Bill Brooks

In his practical, straightforward approach, Brooks directs you through the entire niche selling process. He shows you how to develop workable sales strategies based on customer loyalty, prestige, referrals, and alliances. Discover how to enhance your standing in the minds of prospects and customers using the power of personal positioning.
ISBN: 1-55623-499-6 $24.95

Prices Subject to Change without Notice
Available in fine bookstores and libraries everywhere.

MEGABRANDS
How to Build Them, How to Beat Them
D. John Loden

One of the most significant changes occurring in consumer products marketing today is the consolidation of business in the hands of a few powerful brands. Increasingly, marketers are focusing on growth through line extension due to the high costs—and the high failure rates—of new products. Now, for the first time, *Megabrands* brings together the strategies these powerful brands are using.

In particular, *Megabrands* shows you how to leverage the strength of a brand leader and how to build market share, customer loyalty, and sales. If you're not working for the number one brand, *Megabrands* provides strategies you can use to maximize brand distinctions and overcome the leader's superior resources.

Using schematics and visual aids, author John Loden helps you identify your strengths and your competition's weaknesses. Market leaders can discover where the best opportunities for leveraging exist. Competing brands can locate profitable market niches to dominate.

Conventional wisdom says brand extension is defensive. *Megabrands* shows you how to use brand extension offensively and strengthen your overall business. Using a product development matrix, Loden details how to build an extended product line off an established brand. He also shows you how to:

- Grow, not cannibalize the customer base.

- Implement a systematic approach for increasing the efficiency, not just the level, of marketing spending.

- Provide a base for expansion into new, related categories.

Regardless of your market position, *Megabrands* can help you develop new line extensions. Loden provides case histories on companies that have added value to their brands by extending them. With *Megabrands* as a guide, your business can too!

About the Author...

John Loden is president of FCB HealthCare, the healthcare marketing communications subsidiary of Foote, Cone & Belding Communications. FCB HealthCare is one of the top 10 healthcare agencies in the United States. Prior to joining FCB HealthCare in 1990, Loden was executive vice president of FCB/San Francisco—the largest consumer advertising agency in the West.

In addition to FCB, Loden has held senior management positions in a number of major advertising agencies and client companies, including vice president of J. Walter Thompson, senior vice president of Ally & Gargano, and director of marketing for Bristol Myers Products. He also directed his own New York-based new products consulting firm for several years.

Loden holds a B.A. with honors from Colgate University and did graduate work at the Annenberg School of Communications, University of Pennsylvania.